THE LION PEOPLE

THE LION PEOPLE

Incorporating
THE PASCHAT PAPERS
Intercosmic Messages from the Future

Murry Hope

THOTH PUBLICATIONS

Thoth Publications
64 Leopold Street
Loughborough
LE11 5DN

ISBN 978 1 870450 01 0

Produced in the United Kingdom by Booksprint

DEDICATION

To Martin, whose art work adorns the
cover of this book and other works of mine,
in gratitude and appreciation for his love,
loyalty and unstinting hard work
in the Cause of Light.

ACKNOWLEDGEMENTS

Thanks are due to the BBC for permission to use material
from their Radio 4 broadcast, *Arrows of Time;*
to Leslie Smith, who conducted the interviews,
and to Dr.Lyall Watson for allowing the use
of his excellent quotes.

Photographs have been provided with the
kind permission of the British Museum

CONTENTS

I have come from the house of the Leonine One,
I left there for the house of Isis,
I saw her hidden mysteries in that she let me see
the birth of the Great God.

(Ancient Egyptian Coffin Text)

INTRODUCTION

The story which led to the contents of this book goes back a long, long way to when I was a tiny child – before I could even walk, in fact. I used to have a vague memory of arriving in some inhospitable place far from my native planet, in the company of a group of beings, all of whom were not hominids. No, I had not seen or heard any science fiction; I am not of that generation. Besides, as a young child I was raised by a sound, no-nonsense English nanny and sent to boarding school at the age of eight, during which period the only literature I was exposed to was of a classical nature. I did not surface again until my teens, when there was still a war on. There was no television, of course and I could not afford to go to the cinema, but I still had that memory

It was not until I was fifty years old, during a session of hypnotic regression, that I was able to resolve the enigma and the whole story came tumbling out. I will not bore my readers with those details, however, as the most important thing to emerge from the unblocking of my far memory was the true nature of those beings I vaguely recalled from pre-birth. I later came to know them as the Paschats, or Lion People, and their neighbours as the Ishnaans, or Crystal People. It is their story, cosmic philosophy and teachings that this book is all about.

The name 'Paschat' is guaranteed to evoke a few comments from my more learned friends. After all, *'chat'* is French for cat, and Pasht was another name for the old Egyptian cat goddess, who was also known as Bast or Bastet. But then there are other names for lion gods and goddesses, such as Sekhmet, Shu and Tefnut. Perhaps there is no word in our language to equate with this race of beings, so my subconscious has dredged up a descriptive name to indicate to the best of its ability that there is a resemblance between Paschats and our present day felines.

Or could it be that the ancient Egyptians based many of their beliefs and effigies on descriptions passed on to them from previous generations, the true meaning of these having long since been distorted by the passage of time? But this does not mean that they never existed! How many of us can recall in accurate detail what we did ten years ago? Quite often the emotion of a situation registers in our memory rather than the event itself. Statements uttered under hypnosis frequently leave question marks, even if these simply refer to situations that took place comparatively recently and can therefore be easily verified. So one has to adopt a broad view and assess the facts for oneself.

Many psychiatrists and consultants dismiss the validity of hypnotherapy on the grounds that whatever is dredged up from the subconscious mind has already been written there in the genetic code, and that we are simply probing the lives, works and deeds of our ancestors. On this premise, however, identical twins should, under regression, come up with exactly the same story. But they do not. Neither are they necessarily of identical temperaments. The celebrated American astrologer Stephen Arroyo, in his book *Astrology, Karma and Transformation,* comments on his own twin sisters, born in rapid succession, the ascendants in their charts being only one and a half degrees apart. And yet, although their charts describe them as alike in general ways, they are as different as night and day on a spiritual level. One is esoterically inclined, a vegetarian, interested in astrology and allied New Age subjects; the other is extroverted, with more worldly interests and tastes.

Nor am I alone in my pre-life memories of another world. Recent experiments in hypnotic regression in Soviet Russia revealed that several people experienced recall on a life or lives on other planets and in other lifeforms. I have also received similar confirmation from psychiatrists and psychologists practising in the United States and other parts of this world. The Law of Synchronicity would appear to be operating here, our present age being perhaps the right period for this knowledge to be made generally known.

The following texts constitute a series of dialogues which could broadly be described as 'channelled', but with a difference. The contacts are neither guides, masters, the spirits of deceased relatives, personalities – exalted or otherwise – from the Earth's past, nor extra-terrestrial hominids. They are beings from another time-zone which does not exist concurrently with our own, and which could loosely be described as representing our future.

These intelligences, who are not of the hominid impulse, have, in their own world, reached a scientifically advanced state in which they have gained control over the element of time, so what we are dealing with has no religious, occult or sinister overtones, but simply consists of a telepathic contact with another time-zone, or a mind-to-mind communication in Outer Time.

Although I have always been wary of lending my mind to other essences, I have been forced to admit that one cannot analyze an experience unless one partakes of its content. The late Carl Jung was not afraid to do just this, as may be evidenced in his *VII Sermones ad Mortuos,* and many other of the deeply mystical experiences he unashamedly related in his profound and illuminating works. Besides, my Paschat connection is purely a telepathic one anyway, which process does not involve the relinquishment of my own mental control. Nor am I the only one to effect this connection, as we shall see in later chapters.

My Paschat connection was originally forged in 1980, and the subject matter of our 'dialogues' has supplied me with material for several of my other books and lectures. However, the rapidly escalating decline in spiritual values, coupled with the ethical confusion so prevalent in today's world, has prompted me to share with others that which has afforded me such enlightenment and comfort over the past eight years. Besides, the Paschats themselves have indicated that the time is right and, after all, Time is their primary subject.

At which stage I deem it prudent to hand over to my Paschat friends.

PART I

THE PASCHAT PAPERS

A Cosmic Philosophy from the Future

A series of telepathic dialogues between the
author and leonine aliens from the future.
Recorded from 1980 to 1987.

THE PASCHATS AND CRYSTAL PEOPLE

Allow me to introduce myself, dear things. My name is Kaini, for your convenience pronounced 'Kay-nee'. Who am **I**? **I** am neither spirit guide, godling, nor what you term a master. I do not belong to your time. In your terms of reference I come from the future. One of the things we would like to teach you is the nature and energy of time, and this is your first lesson. But let me start by telling you a story. As I read in your minds that on your planet all good stories commence with a certain phrase, we shall also begin with

Once upon a time there was, still is, and will be for many eons, a solar system that you in your Inner Time have named Sirius, after its major visible star. Over vast periods of Inner Time there have been changes in both the stars and planets in this binary system, but my tale concerns one particular era when a race of beings dwelt on one small planet.

As you see this system at present there are two suns, one small and one large, but this was not always so. There was a time when the smaller star was a yellow sun, not unlike your own luminary, and it was this star-sun that was orbited by the planet on which our species developed. In this cool, well irrigated and highly verdant land there evolved a race of beings whom, for want of a better name, we shall call 'Paschats'.

Our days and nights, however, were very different from yours. We had periods, call them 'days' if you like, that were moderately light and bright, depending on the position of the second star-sun before it collapsed. There were other very bright days indeed during the light of the blue-white star-sun when we were often unable to leave our homes, and also periods of great darkness when everything withdrew into a long sleep or hibernation.

I am from a tribe or group known as the Karidel. There were four basic tribes or races on my old planet, each having its own specific

17

role or duty. As we all understood the principles of archetypal expression and the coming and going of the psyche or essence-fragment there were no bad relations or feelings or resentment between the races. The Karidel were rulers and philosophers, the Orotheta were warriors and protectors, the Paetri were creative artists, artisans and skilled workers, and the Eata were the general folk who fitted in anywhere and who were very, very strong physically.

Our race evolved from a specific cosmic impulse which produces a particular evolutionary strain or genotype. This primary impulse formulated the genetic code that shaped us into the species we ultimately became. For your visualization, the nearest description would be a feline genus appearing as a cross between your domestic cat and the lion family, but our features are more refined. Our jaws are less elongated and our ears less rounded than your lions. We stand erect on two legs as tall or taller than yourselves, our bodies having been adapted to this posture over a long period of time. The males of our species are maned, but not our females. Our paws have also evolved to a more useful shape over long periods of adaptation. In answer to the question I see forming in your mind, yes we do have tails.

We were distinguishable by our colour and eyes. My tribe were brownish or fawn in colour with bright blue eyes. The warriors were orange-eyed and sandy in hue, like your lions or marmalade cats. The artists were pale, white or greyish, and green or turquoise-eyed, while the strong folk were a mixture of all shades, and often striped. When we first started our course of evolution we were fur covered, but later we clothed ourselves for decoration rather than modesty. Our planet was very sparsely inhabited, only certain parts of it being warm enough to live in. One of these belts of vegetation was quite lush, while the other was similar in temperature to parts of northern Europe. Our bodies had evolved to accommodate the temperatures encountered on our native planet, so we managed well.

I would like to give you a little of our history and background so that you have an idea as to what sort of intelligences you are dealing with. Although our role is mainly one of observation we would like to extend a helping hand to you across time, as you will certainly need some external direction in the decades that lie ahead for you.

Paschats do not speak with words or sounds. We are telepathic, which explains why we are able to talk to you through the barriers of space and time. But we were not always so adept at mind-to-mind communication. On our native planet we originally communicated through a series of speech-like sounds, but after our relocation to Ishna, which I shall shortly tell you about, the new atmosphere affected our vocal cords and we found ourselves unable to use our voices as we had done previously, so we developed our own method of silent communication.

In telpathizing with you, Murry, I am limited to the vocabulary and terms of reference available in your conscious and subconscious memory banks, as with anyone else with or through whom I shall be privileged to converse. In years hence, when your planet has made further scientific progress, terms more descriptive and acceptable will become available to beings like myself. Names to us are simply energy frequencies or vibrations, so when it comes to names or titles I shall try to convey them in sound form.

Over extensive periods of Inner Time we evolved both spiritually and somatically, but along rather different lines from our planetary neighbours. You see, in our solar system there was another inhabited planet we call Ishna, that owed its light and life to the large, blue-white star. Those who dwelt thereon were known in cosmic circles as the Crystal People. But it was a long time before we came to meet them, although our astronomers knew of their existence as their astronomers knew of ours.

We lived happily on our small globe, enjoying its fruits and sharing our evolving experience with the other life forms. But as time progressed it was noted by our scientists that the star-sun which gave us light and life had started to undergo drastic changes which, they realized, would be disastrous for us all. But fortunately, by this time, we had established contact with the Crystal People who had started to visit us regularly and to whose planet we also paid frequent visits. As conditions slowly worsened and the force field of our star-sun commenced to widen, our planetary neighbours, in consultation with our own Elders, decided on a drastic but necessary course of action: they would evacuate the whole of our race, and those other lifeforms from our planet that were capable of surviving in the new environment, to their world, for it was realized that the radiation emitted by the yellow starsun during its final collapse would destroy our little sphere and all life thereon.

19

Ishna, however, was a much warmer planet than ours and of a very different atomic and chemical structure. Having long been aware of the impending disaster, they had prepared a domed complex in which the air and temperature had been adjusted to the conditions on our home planet. Fortunately we were not a numerically large population, and neither were the Crystal People, so there was plenty of room for all, their planet being larger than ours.

Very slowly over several generations their scientists acclimatized our bodies to the Iciness atmosphere, which naturally caused mutations. Our coats thinned out and our bodies underwent changes; the skin beneath our fur was of a leathery texture, immensely tough by your standards, but it grew softer. Yet we still retained our physical strength and we could bend one of your steel bars as though it were putty! Of course, our mixed race was the strongest among us. In time we were able to leave our domed complex and step forth into the Iciness world to stand side by side with our new brothers and sisters, yet with each race retaining its own group individuality and skills.

I have lived through many lives and have witnessed the birth, growth and death of other star systems as well as my own; worlds which function at frequencies different from either our own planet, Ishna, or Earth. From your concept of the future I project back into my linear past, which is your present, as do others from future time-zones. Some use mental telepathy, such as we are practising, while there are those who employ advanced technology. A few have actually returned from your own linear future to be born into Earth bodies in your present. I have heard you refer to these as 'old souls', but I prefer the term 'cosmically mature essences', which has no affiliation with any of your major creeds and is therefore less likely to cause confusion.

In quaternary terms we Paschats are of the nature of the elements of Earth and Fire, meaning that we are creative, yet practical and well-grounded race, strong physically and with bodies of a molecular structure not dissimilar to certain creatures on Earth. We mined our native planet, we made things much as you do, built homes in a similar way, and ironed out our differences logically. The Crystal People, on the other hand, are of the nature of the elements of Fire and Air, being intellectual or cerebral, and also highly creative. Their bodies are constructed of a crystalline substance, the like of which would be totally unknown to your chemistry, being very light, fine and fragile. They have little physical strength as you know it, but possess very powerful minds and are highly ingenious.

Paschats breed in much the same way as you do on Earth, but not so the Crystal People. The males and females unite together and shortly afterwards the female brings forth a small egg which is soft when ejected. This is carried carefully to a very important place in every Iciness home, the birth/growth chamber. There it is placed in a special receptacle on what you would probably describe as an altar. As certain aspects are formed between their planet and the star-sun, the two who have created the egg must jointly lay their hands upon it. With each touch a further stage in its growth is attained. As the egg slowly expands the outer casing assumes a crystalline appearance, becoming gradually more transparent until the contents are clearly visible. It would be useless to tell you the time period involved here, as time for them bears no relationship whatsoever to the periods you know as hours, days, months, or years. For the Crystal People it is through the joint efforts of the parents that the egg grows, for without this there would be no growth and no children. At the time of birth the outer structure starts to crumble away to reveal two small beings, for all Iciness children (and all Paschat cubs) are born twins, a fact which did not escape the knowledge of the ancients on your own planet if you care to consult your myths.

Students of Greek mythology will tell you that Zeus visited Leda in the form of a swan, after which she gave birth to four eggs that eventually hatched to produce two sets of twins, Pollux and Helen, and Castor and Clytemnestra. From whence did the Greeks get this idea? From pre-Flood legends that had been passed down to them from Atlantean colonists. These had, in turn, heard the story from their forebears who were visited centuries earlier by the Crystal People and Paschats. This was also why the ancient Egyptians were able to depict us so accurately in their god-forms, and certain of your African tribes still harbour folk memories of our visit.

The numerical balance of the Crystal People is always kept constant. This is achieved by mental processes, and not clinically. Thus the balance and distribution of usefulness amongst the people is always as it should be, the type of children to be born being chosen by the parents and engineered by genetic selection. Nor is this process simply geared to the needs of the economy or social structure, for it also accommodates the evolutionary requirements of the incoming psyche or that particular fragment of the whole essence so that it, too, can express its individuality in a caring and complementary manner.

The Crystal People are what you would describe as fair in colouring, although their skin is more of a golden or yellow tone. Their eyes are slanted and either golden in colour or deep grey flecked with gold. Their hair is very white, but it is not of the same texture as yours being more like fine glass threads. Again I seek out words for expression from within your mind, but find there are none appropriate. So I must leave it with you to visualize. Their males and females are so alike as to be indistinguishable to your eyes.

And so, from the confines of the Ishnaan planet the scientists of the Crystal People and the Paschats jointly reached into outer space. On one such journey into the vast beyond, using the combined impetus of time energy and anti-matter to cross timezones, one of our craft suffered a malfunction and the expedition was forced to land on an alien planet in a strange and hitherto uncharted solar system.

But, as you probably know, nothing really happens by chance and the Old Ones who created the universe, and to whom we turn for spiritual guidance, explained to us how the future of our two solar systems were inextricably linked, for it was on your then youthful planet that our lost craft had landed. Of course, those who were involved in that first contact knew nothing of the overall plan. But later, other Paschats and Crystal People visited your Earth and certain of these, and others, have since taken on Earth bodies from time to time to concern themselves with your planet's evolutionary development.

I have not been an Earth person myself. Paschats do not take easily to lives in Earth bodies, although this can occur on rare occasions. We are more likely to enter the body of one of your more highly developed domestic cats, and then usually for a specific purpose: to be near to a loved one, or as a protector and guardian against those negative forces that surround your planet.

You will not see me or the people from my time-zone while you are in your present body, Murry, but then for you is that really necessary? Eventually your people will learn to move from one time-zone to another at will. Then we shall meet Earthlings 'in person', as you say.

Episodes of time exist one within the other, just as there are microbes living on your bodies that you neither see, feel, nor are consciously aware of. Take a closer look through your instruments, however, and you will observe that these organisms are very much alive. There are innumerable beings in other timezones throughout the universe; some of these zones are interrelated, some are not. Many life forms, like your own, are totally unaware of the existence of others yet are observed with ease by those who are able to negotiate the time barrier. These zones may crisscross and overlap with your own, but you will be no more aware of them than you are of the X-rays that your medical people pass through your bodies.

Different impulses strike the cosmos at varying times creating diverse life forms. Your genotype is but one of millions! But all do not 'take' on any one planet. Conditions offered for somatic growth and development are the deciding factors as to which evolutionary strains eventually survive and dominate. On Earth the impulse that 'took' in the strongest way and retained its evolutionary hold was the one you call *Homo sapiens,* although man was by no means the first. (Should I use the term 'man' from time to time in these dialogues I will be referring to the collective, and not merely the male of the species.) Hominids are primarily watery or emotional by nature, your bodies and the planet upon which you live being composed predominantly of this element.

Since the connection between your solar system and ours is a strong one, many archetypal names and principles that have become meaningful to you over the ages have their roots with us. The diversity of beliefs on your planet has led to the bestowal of many names – mythological, religious or pantheistic – but all relating to similar principles.

Murry, I have heard you use the term 'Outer Time' to indicate a state or condition of existence which is not regulated by the movement of your planet or the hands of your clocks, and which may be negotiated during sleep state or when experiencing altered states of consciousness. There are indeed frequencies in the universe which accommodate eternity in that they encompasses the past, present and future, but in the state of true timelessness all exists in the Eternal Now. However, your people have not yet reached that stage of understanding where they can readily accept or absorb this concept, although glimmers of this truth are beginning to dawn in some human minds. During these communications others in addition to myself will be with you from Outer Time. In your understanding you might say that some are more advanced than I, but from where we are we do not see things in these rather black and white terms. What you term 'advancement' only pertains to different time-zones and their proximity to the Centre Point. Those from a time-zone nearer to the Centre than mine can see and understand more of the universe than I can. I, in turn, looking back in time to you see more than you do. But even though I am familiar with the time circuits in the universe, how to operate them and the experience to be gained from them, I am by no means all-knowing.

To some of you the idea of what you term a 'godhead' is an ultimate state of perfection. To us, however, it is all time in one, the Eternal Now or Centre Point from which all time-zones radiate into infinity. It is instantaneously in touch with all that any other time-zone embraces throughout eternity, having no beginning or end. And yet even this is not an accurate description as it suggests a geometrical paradigm and pinpoints a location. The Centre Point has no fixed place in the universe that you would conceive of as 'heaven'.

Although a certain amount of wisdom has percolated through from your early races, a great deal has become lost or obscured so there is much for us to discuss as our dialogues progress, for I do not wish this to be a one-sided discourse. We Paschats are poor preachers and such is not our calling.

After certain events have taken place on your world our task will have been fulfilled. Then both Crystal People and Paschats, including those who are at present in Earth bodies, will return to our own time-zone for the next stage of our spiritual development.

So I, Kaini, became involved with your planet. No, I was not among those who first landed, but I have been appointed by the Old Ones to watch over those who originally came from our solar system who are involved in the growth, development and forthcoming evolutionary changes on Earth, my role being often described by your early civilizations as 'tutelary guardian'. Your ancients designated two deities as guardians of the sacred places. Observe that they are depicted as the twin lion gods of Yesterday and Today; in other words, *time!*

We guard diligently, and do not in our vigilance ever interfere unless…! We are silent watchers and thus we protect, but when it becomes necessary for us to strike in defence it is with the strength of the lion and the skill and speed of the cheetah.

So, in that safe knowledge I will end episode one of my story, a strange one perhaps, but one that will slowly unfold to you a philosophy of time appropriate to the evolution of your planet.

****

QUESTION: Did you have any other life forms that you could communicate with on your planet?

ANSWER: It depends upon which planet you mean. On the old Paschat planet there were other life forms which we considered as our equals. There was a form of intelligent plant life that was not limited in movement as are the plant kingdoms on your planet. Our 'plant people' could take up their own roots, move around, and put them down in some other place providing the right kind of soil was available. These kindly beings would visit our homes and stay with us, as every Paschat dwelling had what, for want of a better term, I would call 'garden patches' where a visiting plant person could put down roots for the night, or stay longer if it so wished. In return for our hospitality they would give us their fruits, nuts, berries or healing leaves, so that we were never obliged to deprive them of their life in order to obtain our own sustenance. Many of these plant people liked to live in small colonies which we Paschats could always visit when we needed food, which they willingly provided.

Our trees were both our best friends and our oracles, and we would have long, telepathic discourses with them. Unlike the plant people, however, they did stay rooted to one spot. In the area from which my tribe came there was a tree of great antiquity that would rest for long periods and then awaken to dispense great wisdom, learning and healing.

There were also the friendly water serpents whose eggs, which they

25

gave to us freely, constituted our main source of protein. Many species of birds lived with and around us, in fact all life forms blended harmoniously together and enjoyed perfect telepathic communication one with another.

On the Ishnaan planet there are small lizard-like animals that are very gentle and several other species you would not recognize.

QUESTION: You say that a few of the Crystal People are incarnate in Earth bodies at present, but that the Paschats do not usually take on hominid form although there can be the odd exception. Why is this?

ANSWER: The Crystal People emanated from a hominid impulse, which means that they are basically of human type, although the components. of their bodies are different from yours. Their basic elemental qualities are of Fire and Air, which metaphysically represent creativity and intellect. If and when they do assume Earth bodies it is likely to be in highly creative or cerebral modes as would manifest in the composition of music, or the disciplines of medicine or scientific discovery. The fields of higher mathematics could also prove fruitful for them, but they are less likely to appear in the humanities than might be expected. The reason for this is that they function best in more rarified, academic atmospheres where they can create new ideas and themes for their stronger, more physically active disciples to carry out. They will be the originators of advanced metaphysical concepts, and of greater breadths of understanding in philosophy, science and religion. But they are not necessarily the faces that adorn your media, as they tend to be private, rather shy people.

Now Paschats are a different proposition. Although we are physically stronger than the Crystal People, our strength is genetically programmed to suit our particular type of feline body. A Paschat incarnating into a hominid form would find coordination difficult and the human body would not afford the degree of physical strength to which we are accustomed. This would tend to confine our activities and abilities to the area of the mind, which could give rise to many problems, frustrations and idiosyncrasies. Not that these would be impossible to handle through mental discipline, but a certain amount of suffering would result. A Paschat incarnating into a female human body might well be incapable of reproduction due to incompatibilities between the frequencies of the feline essence and the functioning of the human female pituitary system. Being of a leonine nature, Paschats are naturally given to extraversion, openheartedness and a degree of theatricality, which we would find difficult to express easily in an alien environment. Remember also that we are a very tribal people, used to a set and preselected way of life, so we would experience insecurity problems on a planet such as Earth where there is so much confusion and uncertainty. Although many of you may view your native felines as 'loners', this is not really the case. A cat spends much time out of its body and would feel very lonely indeed without those sleep periods during which it is able to make contact with the rest of its spiritual tribe or pride.

But I will tell you there are a few Paschats on your Earth at the moment. These are the scribes of our race, who are there to record for us first hand the experiences undergone during the Earth's evolutionary interchanges, or 'quantum leaps' I believe you call them. We, in our time-zone, naturally keep a careful watch over their safety, although we may not, by Cosmic Law, offer them any advantages over their 'fellow men'. In other words, they must fend for themselves as do all intelligences incarnate on your planet.

QUESTION: Are there intelligences from other parts of the universe, as well as yourselves from the Sirius system, who are trying to help us here on Earth through the difficult days that we are told lie ahead? If so, who are they and where are they from?

ANSWER: There are indeed those who look in from other time-zones, some out of mild curiosity; others, like ourselves, are anxious to be of assistance; and a few are of less kindly intent. We do not have close communications with all of these intelligences, but we do know the Dolphin people and the Lizard beings from the Capella/Auriga region, among others.

Like ourselves, the latter also visited your planet thousands of years ago, even before we did, but their efforts to help the species existing there in those times failed, which greatly distressed them. The evolutionary pattern was corrected with the passing of the saurians, however. These people are benign and gentle beings but because their evolutionary type is so far removed from your own they could appear frightening to your peoples. Now the Crystal

27

People are very beautiful by your standards of beauty and would not, were you to meet them, present a fearful picture.

I can hear you asking: "What about Paschats?" When the time comes for our time-zones to intermingle, those who are around then will meet a fine looking, handsome bunch of felines, with a special sense of humour that is peculiar to our kind! It is not a cruel humour that brings smiles at the expense of another's tears, however. Anyone who likes felines will like Paschats. I think you would consider us cuddly by your standards.

TIME

In order to progress to the next stage of development, both scientifically and spiritually, the peoples of Earth need to project their minds beyond the confines of their own planet so that, in viewing it from afar they tan gain a clearer perspective. To achieve this new outlook they must negotiate time in order to observe how evolutionary patterns are formed over immense periods of Inner Time to produce instant results in Outer Time.

But is this really as complex as it sounds? Not at all. It is simply a question of programming the human brain to compute the fact that differing time-zones tan exist side by side or one within the another, as maybe observed in dreams which frequently involve intertime-zone experiences.

You have a saying, "God is everywhere." You could substitute the word 'time' for 'god' because there is a point in Outer Time that embraces all time, but with due respect to your theologies it does not consist of a single, throned deity. Rather it is a complexity of intelligences or essences bound into one harmonious thought. Some of your theologies teach that you are all gods in the making; in a sense this is nearer the actual truth.

Although I am from your future I do not yet know the whole truth, however, nor does anyone from my time-zone, nor anyone on your planet at present. My Teacher knows more than I, and it is from him that I have learned about those time-zones that I have not as yet experienced. There have been those who have incarnated on your planet from the future whom your people have sometimes hailed as masters, teachers or saints. Sadly, you often destroy their bodies because the message they give disturbs the comfort of your conditioned thinking patterns. But their essences continue forever and a time will tome, perhaps years ahead in your Inner Time (but 'now' in Outer Time), when your errors will become apparent and you will adjust your ethics to accommodate the virtues of tolerance and understanding. Sadly, however, many who are incarnate on your planet have become locked in restricted time circuits and cannot see any further than that which is relative to their immediate well being, family strut tune, personal gratification or physical satisfaction. But as more amongst you become aware of the existence of the timeless state, the doors of knowledge will start to open for you and your perspective will slowly broaden.

Many of you are questioning why it is only now that certain information, such as the structure and role of minute particles, is coming to light. I have even heard it suggested the people always find what they are looking for when they start to look for it. The statement "seek and ye shall find" intimates that everything you can imagine is already in existence, so that it appears to take life from your very imagination. But which way round is it really? May we suggest that every possible permutation of experience, life, and beingness *ad infinitum* already exists or is being played out in another time-zone and when people are ready to accept this or that snippet of information they will find it simply by opening their minds to the concept of its existence.

Let us take a look at the metaphysical aspects. Some of those who follow spiritualism are often heard to remark that this or that guide does not believe in reincarnation, as though a belief in something were a prerequisite for its existence. Any communicator who confesses to having a limited knowledge or experience of Outer Time is admitting to his or her own development level. In my case, for example, by my very lack of knowledge beyond a certain stage I pinpoint my position on the evolutionary ladder, which emphasizes the fact that I have not yet reached that Centre Point that you call the Godhead.

When referring to the intelligence that motivates your body and the various levels of its manifestation you have many terms: soul, spirit, ego, etheric body, astral body, or whatever, according to your religious or philosophical persuasion. I would like to dispense with all these and describe that spark as the 'essence', and its manifestation in fragment form as the 'psyche'.

Many of the terms you employ in metaphysical parlance – 'astral' and 'etheric planes', 'vibrations', 'higher' or 'lower' levels, 'brotherhoods of light', etc. – are but descriptions of what we know as 'time-zones'. Our advice would be to wipe your slates clean and stop trying to over-categorize everything, because many of these terms only engender resentment in younger psyches and a sense of alienation in their spiritually older brethren. Try substituting the words 'aware' and 'more aware', for what you call a higher level merely refers to a time-zone encompassing a wider and more comprehensive field of experience. The ultimate time-zone, or Centre Point, is active/passive, male/female, quaternionic, and embraces all archetypes, including those unfamiliar to your evolutionary strain. All life forms can find their own god or goddess by seeking the archetypal or elemental force within that Centre Point which corresponds to their own unique spark.

From the aforesaid you have no doubt gathered that there is no point at which the evolving essence suffers annihilation. The process of individuation from its originating collective provides the psyche with the impetus which carries it along the linear or Inner Time path of return to the more subtle realms, and thence to its creative source.

The nearer that any form of life or intelligence gets to the Centre Point the more understanding and true knowledge it has access to and the wiser it becomes, as it can see more of the whole picture. Every living thing – each person, plant, stone, planet, star and all that is accommodated thereon or therein – contains an aspect of the central creative force. In order to make contact with that Essence you need to know your individual Self. We will teach you how to find your own Personal Symbol, and your God Symbol which is your time-track to the Centre Point and, although your comprehension of that Centre will be governed by your stage of awareness, this does not mean that even the least experienced of any of us, or the youngest psyche may not reach out. What each of you sees and learns through practising the exercises we will give you will be personal to you and as valid an experience as anyone else's.

It is a great pity that over the years of Inner Time on your planet some of you have found it necessary to give vent to your religious insecurities by persecuting those whose concept of the Centre Point does not correspond with or complement your own. Sad! Perhaps when Earth technology and scientific research finally open the doors to other dimensions, which we know they will, mankind will overcome this streak of intolerance that shackles him to Inner Time.

The tendency among most of you is to look at time as starting with a given event – for example, the so-called 'Big Bang' – and proceeding forward in a straight line. Time is *not* linear: it curves. Even those amongst you who consider yourselves enlightened and who discuss reincarnation in eager tones make the linear mistake. You say, "I had a bad life in 1400, but since then I've made up for it." Because you see a situation from the standpoint of Inner Time, it appears to you that your psyche commenced its journey in the past and progressed towards the future. But as viewed from the Centre Point you and all other life forms experience in the Eternal Now. I have also heard time referred to as a spiral, but even this is not strictly accurate because a spiral goes somewhere. Time is simply an energy which manifests according to the nature, density and frequency of the force fields which pass through it.

I often hear you refer to those intelligences who are very near to the Centre Point as 'Masters' or 'Illumined Ones'. One of the hallmarks of an old, time-travelled essence is a deep understanding of the suffering of others and an ability to communicate that understanding through love. The banner or flag under which such a being may choose to acknowledge the Centre Point is irrelevant, as they have been known to shelter conveniently under the umbrella of your orthodoxy if that would enable them to get on with the task of caring and loving.

As I scan the minds of future readers of these scripts I see confusion regarding the term 'Centre Point', for this might imply to them a fixed position which would clash with my description of a limitless, timeless state. It is simply a term of convenience that I have used to try to convey the concept of a central source from which issue an infinite number of life forms designed to experience on an infinite number of levels, thus continually adding to the original source. But as this source is itself a state of timelessness, all experiences that are undergone in closed time circuits, while these may appear time-bound by the experiencing fragments in question, are instantaneously known and felt in the Outer Time oneness of the initial creative impulse that you would refer to as 'God', or the 'Goddess', depending upon your persuasion.

There are many time-zones which even I cannot conceive of; some involve dense matter, some do not; some pass one through another like your X-rays; while others are parallel to your own world. It is possible to negotiate these zones while in sleep state, but when awake most of you cannot perceive anything around you other than that which vibrates at the same frequency as your own and is therefore visible to you either with the naked eye or through sensitive instruments. Animals, strangely enough, are not thus blinded. In fact, many of them are nearer to the Centre Point than large numbers of your own people. But since you are given to judging evolution by intellectual standards of achievement, your yardsticks are materialistic ones and do not apply in other time-zones. The ability to build a house of bricks, work through a page of mathematics, or construct deadly weapons of destruction are not valid criteria for judging the wisdom of an evolving essence.

The majority of you, like many of those guides or deceased relatives you believe in, do not have access to the experiences of your other fragments. The human brain was originally designed to accommodate a series of evolutionary programmes that would carry it through from the primitive to the more advanced stages of somatic experience, and when a certain area of that organ is stimulated the faculty of inter-time sight becomes activated. Although this is not likely to occur worldwide until certain future events have transpired, there are a few among you who have already experienced this development. Mature psyches are able to handle the results. But when the mutation occurs in those who are cosmically younger, they frequently either lack the logic to assess and control it or the cosmic awareness to carry them sanely through its development in the prevailing climate of prejudiced opinion.

One of your television writers invented a character called 'Dr. Who' for the entertainment of children, and since this time traveller first put in an appearance others have elaborated on his adventures. Although these stories contain a grain of truth they are technologically overstated, for mind power will ultimately supercede all 'nuts and bolts' technology.

Dr. Who, like his Star Trek counterparts, finds himself in many periods of history, both on your planet and other worlds, and escapes his assailants in ingenious ways, much to the delight of old and young amongst you. Beings from the future can incarnate into past epochs in your linear time, although certain periods are difficult for the evolved psyche or time traveller to negotiate, for the experience they afford is too limiting for any positive achievement in the spiritual sense. A mature fragment or psyche, for example, would not be drawn to incarnate into a race of primitive barbarians whose only pleasure was slaughter and torture.

****

QUESTION: If it takes millions of years to evolve in Inner Time, and those involved in this evolutionary cycle see time purely as linear, how can this equate with an Eternal Now, at which point you tell us everything happens at once?

ANSWER: Time is relative. Consider the speed of thought, which is infinitely faster than anything you can conceive of in your present methods of propulsion. An essence that is near to the Centre Point can create a thought in less than a microsecond, and in that instant a billion year Inner Time evolutionary cycle takes place somewhere in the universe. There comes a point at which an essence-fragment evolving through an Inner Time sequence becomes aware of Outer Time while still functioning within those Inner Time limitations. Your Earth is nearing that period and, when it is reached, communications with other time-zones will become common practice. But first of all you will need to learn how to harness the forces of Outer Time, which you will do in due course.

QUESTION: Astronomy has recently shown us that quasars a long way away are receding at a speed near to that of light, and that they will soon reach that point in linear time at which scientists reckon that the universe began from one Big Bang. Is this true?

ANSWER: In part, yes. But then they are only viewing the material universe, which is but one of many. This is because they are only able to observe that which resonates at frequencies detectable by their existing technology.

The Big Bang theory is much cherished by many of your astronomers and astrophysicists, but again it is only part of the story. The universe breathes in and out from the Centre Point, alternately indrawing and receding with each inhalation and exhalation. When matter travels at the speed of light or faster, subtle changes are effected in its structure and nature. In other words it begins to penetrate other finer and less obvious dimensions. This might prove incomprehensible to many who have been programmed to one linear time-zone.

There have indeed been Big Bangs in past linear time, but not one of these actually started the universe. The universe which is visible to you comes into being when cosmic matter that has been indrawn to a single coalesced state reaches a critical mass and once more explodes outwards, this being part of the continuing evolutionary process. The time scale your scientists are at present viewing as representing the beginning of the universe is but one exhalation that manifested in the worlds of dense matter, or what you would perceive as solid form. In time you will come to understand the nature of anti-matter, but that is another subject.

QUESTION: If you are from the future you must know what is going to happen here on Earth over the next few years. Why don't your people intervene and stop wars and famines?

ANSWER: Because nothing would be achieved if we did. It is all rather like the sickness and cure we shall be telling you about shortly. Unless people understand why they are acting in a certain way, or why they decide to cease those actions, they will not be ready to venture into Outer Time for they would only prove a nuisance to themselves and others. If you stop a child experiencing such things as disagreements with other children, fights, squabbles, jealousies, etc., and shield it from its own faults – selfishness, bigotry, persecution of the weak – it will never learn and will only prove an even greater menace to society in adulthood.

If you are to stop fighting each other, erecting foolish boundaries, starving large numbers of your people, and treating so atrociously the other life forms with which you share your planet, it must be because you understand *why* you are ceasing to perpetrate these misdeeds and *not* because a people with a superior technology stand over you and threaten to turn a super ray on anyone who falls out of line. Discipline must be self-imposed to be truly effective; when it is imposed by an external force it does not really teach and only pushes the imbalances even deeper into the psyche. Disciplinary measures are good for the very young until they can learn to distinguish for themselves between that which is Cosmic Law and that which is not cosmically correct. But the day must come when the child becomes the adult, at which point self-discipline must start. No, we of the future *cannot* interfere with the past. What we do is to stand by as those in the transition stage slowly become aware of Outer Time and lend a helping hand at their rebirth into these new realms of consciousness.

QUESTION: But surely if you are able to travel from the future into the past, seeing the mess man has made of things, could you not rectify man's mistakes and so change the future?

ANSWER: Not at the level at which it has occurred. One of your mystics once wrote: "God does not reverse the law of gravity to prevent one man from committing suicide," the consequences being obvious.

Let us say, for example, that a train crashes because an error of judgment has been made. In another, or parallel, time dimension those same people will travel on that train, but in that dimension a mistake will not be made and no-one will leave incarnation. Everything is relative to what you are experiencing in any one time-zone and, believe me, you are by no means limited to what you see around you! Equally, you may experience in one time-zone that which appears exactly the same as another in dress, housing, motor cars, customs, and so forth, but with subtle differences. In one you may lose a leg in a crash while in the other, which is fractionally different, you may survive intact. One life may see you rich and enjoying every luxury, another may see you in dire poverty.

Mature essence-fragments may elect to enter a time-zone which affords them alternative experiences of the kind that a younger fragment would not be able to handle. Or they may choose to negotiate these during sleep state to test their own strength of mind and rationale.

Familiarity with present day conditions, *déjà vu,* is simply an indication of existing experiences being lived in another very close or even parallel time-zone. Memory is not limited to the linear past; equally, you can remember the future and the present. Dimensions of time often interweave and there are points or warps where the framework between two or more timezones is fragile. This can give rise to strong imprints from a former period which are commonly known as 'haunting'. It can also account for missing people who are accidentally projected into another time-zone, but even that constitutes a valid experience for the person in question. The natural structural barriers between bands of time can also be affected by strong emotional impacts, as with localities where much suffering or personal shock has taken place.

All these things will become increasingly apparent to you as your technology advances. Instruments fine enough to perceive subtle changes will open up new territories for the human mind to investigate and conquer. But be sure that you anchor such findings to a sound cosmic philosophy, or you will lose all moral sense and cause yourselves much suffering.

No doubt some of you are thinking, "But if we can return to any time-zone to re-experience, does it really matter whether we are good or evil?" To the universe, of course, it does not. But to you yourselves, yes, it does! **I will** try to explain to you a little about the force engendered by what you term 'evil' in later communications.

You all have a latent power for enquiry, the pursuit of knowledge, self-help, caring for others, and love. If you learn to use these gifts yourselves, instead of always looking for someone to help, guide, or lead you, you will branch out into time-consciousness with skill, ease and safety. But for so many centuries you have relied upon mystiques built up by this tradition or that religion, this system or that discipline, that you have limited your spiritual resources to the confines of the power generated by previous followers of those paths. Your propensity for personal defence has been stifled because you have lost your cosmic identity and, being blind to the existence of other dimensions beyond your own planet, you are therefore unaware of the true nature of the Centre Point.

EARTH

Your planet Earth has been passing through a painful stage of growth that could be likened to a very unhappy family in which there is discord between the parents and disharmonious relationships with other members and branches of the family. Everything within that family structure is chaos: the home is dirty and uncared for, food is lacking in nourishment and most times scarce; there is brutality; love and care are conspicuously absent.

Yet, as your own psychologists often note, the members of such a family appear to cling together as though forming a rearguard against an external world that might, for all they know, be even more hostile than their own wretched existence. So, if some kindly soul from outside that family offers a helping hand, either through advice or material assistance, the reception can be hostile in the extreme. He could be told to mind his own business and the whole family might turn on him.

This is what has happened on your Earth. Many from time to time (or should I say from other time-zones) have tried to help you to put things right, but their efforts have met with rebuff and their bodies murdered. However, the time has now arrived for the teenagers of that family to leave the parental roof and face the outside world, for which affray they prepare themselves with the bravado of bitter resentment tinged with anarchy. But deep down within the minds of many is the knowledge that the world outside could conceivably be better than the one they would be leaving; that in the `Great Beyond' they might be shown the correct way to treat their bodies, have respect and care for others, gather their food humanely, and find peace of mind and spiritual harmony. Any transition can prove frightening for even the stoutest heart, for it represents the unknown as against the known, which is at least familiar for all its squalor.

Many of the people of Earth have reached this state of cosmic adolescence. Some have looked to science and humanism for the answers to their origins and purpose, while others who have realized the limitations of outmoded religious superstitions have already turned to metaphysics, parapsychology, strange cults and the like, their search for cosmic roots taking them into the highways and byways of interplanetary and even interstellar thinking.

When we Paschats and Crystal People took this same step, which we did in generations past in our Inner Time, we did not have the element of fear to contend with, as you have on your planet, for our worlds were not 'fallen' places. In other words, the dual energies of darkness and light had remained in balance for us and, although many of our people did not fully understand Time, the principle had been taught to us through many lives by the Old Ones and those who served them.

Had you on Earth been blessed with cosmically wise parents, you would leave home during spiritual adolescence with peace and inner security. No fears would accompany your steps away from the family door, and no aggressions would dominate your thoughts as you faced the unknown. True security can only come from within. On Earth this is difficult for any of you to find no matter what the age of your psyche. Only with a clear realization of your own individual essence, as a unit of unique existence within this universe, will you be able to link with the eternal flame from which that spark was born and so eliminate fear and insecurity.

Of course it is difficult for you. We Paschats do not have the same problems to cope with as you do, but then you do not *have* ours either! We teachers experience through the comings and goings, the ups and downs, the tears and joys of our pupils, for the individual development of those with whom we communicate is important to us.

There is a saying in one of your religious books about no sparrow falling without the Creator being aware of it. How true! The closer one is to the Centre the more one is able to love and understand those on the outer perimeters. While many are nearer to the Centre than we, the hunger that gnaws at the belly of the starving lion and the searing pain of the captured prey are equally known to us, and for both we weep.

But perhaps you will fall into the category of those adolescents who, metaphorically speaking, do take the plunge, leave home and set up in a place of their own. At first they run home to their mother with their washing and abandon their apartment every time an argument or upsetting problem arises in their lives. But slowly they come to grips with the situation. They start to stand on their own feet and take care of their own things; and when emotions misfire they talk it out with friends. The parents then assume their rightful place as persons to be respected, visited occasionally and watched over in old age, while retaining their love and affection.

I would like to comment on certain religious and occult beliefs concerning numerical significances associated with different hierarchical systems. Is there a 'Sacred Seven', a 'Council of Nine', a 'Holy Trinity', 'Twenty-four Elders round the Throne', a 'Great White Brotherhood'? Well, it all depends from where you are viewing.

From my own viewpoint the answer must, of course, be *no!* There is no numerical limitation in the universe – it is infinite! All conscious life evolves to the Centre Point, be it rocks, plants, hominids, or Paschats! Nor do these different impulses normally intermix, especially in their immature modes. I have never incarnated as an Earth person, so I cannot be labelled 'Julius Caesar' or anything as amusing, although, as I have already explained, some Crystal People have taken Earth bodies, and on very rare occasions so have certain Paschats.

I know of planets where the hominid impulse is dominant, from which places essence-fragments have come to incarnate into Earth bodies for experience. Each of these planets has its own concept of the Centre, its own name for the deity, and when these psyches do incarnate on your Earth they tend to bring through with them past religious race memories that slowly surface and appear as a new faith or philosophy. I can think of a planet in another galaxy that functions on the '9' principle, having nine names for the Centre, or 'God' as you call it, and I can also think of a '3' solar system that has been closely associated with the evolution of Earth.

On your planet you should give more consideration to the number '4', as hominid essence-fragments should have a fourfold nature which takes shape, or which they evolve into, as they attain cosmic maturity. The elements of Air, Fire, Earth and Water, of which your

41

bodies are composed, represent certain principles that have to be understood and controlled. The intellect, creativity, practicality and emotions need to be harnessed and delicately balanced out over many time-zones. Those psyches who have just learned to master one element tend to spend a whole lifetime glorying in that mastery.

Let us consider the case of a man who has recently come to terms with the acquisitive and practical element of Earth. He may follow this with a life in which he excels in all things associated with that elemental principle before proceeding to another more difficult incarnation in which he has to face the challenge of the next element. A successful banker or financier would fall into this category, one with the Midas touch for whom everything turns to gold. People may specialize in a life of money making, or creativity, or intellectual achievement, or emotional fulfilment, but it is not a hallmark of wisdom to be materially successful or proficient in the qualities of one element only! *The truly balanced being is familiar with all, but specializes in none!*

The converse also applies. To ignore one aspect of life denotes an imbalance, so the mature psyche does not neglect, illfeed, or inadequately clothe his or her body, but keeps it clean, warm, fit, and sensibly fed, avoiding extremes of any kind. Because, dear things, this attitude indicates that he or she understands the nature of the four elements of which that body is composed, and pays due deference to their feelings and expression via the matter or molecular structure of that vehicle.

If people from a distant planet were to land on your Earth in the country you call Italy and ask about religion they would be presented with a Roman Catholic programme. Three persons, they would be told, care for our universe: a Father figure, his Son, and a Holy Spirit. No Mother, I'm afraid, which is their sad loss, although they compensate somewhat for this lack of basic polarity with the 'Virgin' Mary.

Were you to meet the people from the region of Orion, they would tell you a very different story about who runs the universe and why. And yet, is their interpretation more valid than yours, or yours that more accurate than theirs? Neither is correct, but points that could be raised in favour of both are that: (1) each creates an ethical code on which the evolving psyche can strap hang until it finds the confidence to assume individual responsibility; and (2) the existence of a Centre Point or godhead of ultimate truth and understanding is at least conceded. But until you are part of that godhead you will never know its true nature.

Many of those who communicate to the peoples of Earth by psychic or telepathic means, and this goes for us also as one cannot make exceptions, know little more than you do. As I explained to you at the commencement of these communications, we are people from the future; we are not 'gods', although your primitives might once have labelled us as such. Our vistas are broader than your present one, that is all. Like attracts like, and those on Earth who are reaching out into space and time for answers will get them from their own kind. Those who hailed from the regions of Andromeda will receive inspiration from their group intelligences from those time-zones. Likewise those from Auriga, Orion, or Sirius. If you want to know about the communicators, enquire a little more deeply about those with whom they communicate.

REINCARNATION

All time exists simultaneously, and yet there is the illusion of passing through it either forward or backward according to the context or given stage of consciousness in which the experience is taking place. This must sound rather like one of those 'mysteries' that you are constantly being asked to accept on religious grounds that appear to have no basis in Earth logic. Now, hold your fire before you condemn the idea out of hand, because your own scientists are well on the way to presenting you with the correct equation for timelessness! In fact, there are those working in higher mathematics who already have a broad understanding of the principles involved.

You proceed through a series of experiences in different dimensions of consciousness, always advancing towards the Centre Point at which all time-zones merge. And yet even this is an illusion for time does not really radiate out in any given direction, pattern or geometric design; it just *is!* However, we have chosen the Centre Point concept for the purpose of conveying the idea to those who have not been conditioned to inter-time thinking. Of course, the fact that you are unaware of other time circuits does not mean that they do not exist! Not all of you are able to observe Outer Time, either through what are generally termed 'psychic faculties' or ESP, or dreams. And, of course, there will be many who will refuse to acknowledge the existence of anything that might upset the cosiness of their present neatly structured thought processes.

Those who do find the time concept difficult to accept would be best advised to leave it alone. Not every mind will be able to compute it, and for many the present may seem enough to cope with. So don't try to imagine you are simultaneously living in the reign of Charles II, the Egypt of 3000 BC, and in a colony on the planet Pluto in 25000 A.D., or the mental fuses could well blow! Other facets of time are not always totally relevant to your present life and there will be those who will feel far more secure if they close their minds to Outer Time experiences in preference to the Now. On the other hand, there will be many who *will* want to know.

Even a simple subject like reincarnation can bring to the fore a host of hidden fears, most of which stem from environmental programming or conventional modes of thinking, but which bear no relationship at all to Cosmic Laws or the way things really are in the universe beyond your small planet. For example, while many females amongst you have no difficulty in accepting the idea that their other fragments might well experience in the male gender, there are numerous males to whom the thought of a life as a woman would prove abhorrent! The male and female principle does not always function in other time-zones in the same way that it does on Earth. The Law of Polarity, however, does apply universally, this being concerned with cosmic force fields and the basic nature of the essence as related to those fields, rather than the physical forms that may be adopted in any given time circuit.

If you come to terms with the existence of Outer Time you will be able to utilize the concept to eliminate that which you most dread; fear of missing out on something – fame, family, wealth, all of which may be yours in another time-zone; fear of the unknown – you are part of the Centre which knows all, so the potential to know and understand lies within each of you; fear of death – which is simply passing from one time-zone to another.

Many of the essence-fragments at present incarnate on your Earth are from different time-zones or parts of the universe. To add to the confusion, there is also a great disparity in what you would call the 'soul-age' of your people, which ranges from the mature to the very young, with the majority falling somewhere in between. There are several reasons why your planet has become a gathering place for such a wide section of cosmic experience, one being the leap forward in time consciousness that is due to occur during the next cosmic age. A mature psyche, or essence-fragment from what you think of as the future, may feel ill at ease in an Inner Time zone that is backwards from its viewpoint, because its values will differ from those currently observed by the collective. But it can and will survive if it is not put to death by those cosmically or spiritually younger than itself.

46

Group Entity intelligences that develop closely in one time-zone will be drawn together in others. If the knowledge of Outer Time is already there within your subconscious mind this whole philosophy will come easily to you, but those with no depth of time experience will find it difficult to accept.

Unless programmed from childhood, the younger psyche finds it difficult to cope with the concept of timelessness. Your science fiction writers are, fortunately, doing a fairly good job here, although we wish that some of their ideas of us 'aliens' were not so fear-inducing and negative. The immature psyche often advertises its soul age with the statement: "It cannot be because I have not experienced it."

Evolutionary progress is also non-linear and the evolving essence can crisscross time circuits, often appearing to double back on itself. Although you may appear to have had incarnations relative to the past history of your planet in terms of Inner Time, this is not strictly accurate. What happens is that you move around time: through it, along it, seeking here and there like a small child wandering across a field of flowers, gathering a white one here, a few blue ones there; "Ouch, some nettles, watch the muddy patch by the stream and the big creepy-crawly under the stone." Another analogy would be a play that has already been written with a set of archetypal characters. You engage in the performance of certain of those roles at different times, giving them your own unique interpretation to the extent that from time to time the play itself may sometimes seem to change its message. And yet, the overall story is, like Cosmic Law, constant at all levels.

****

QUESTION: I am puzzled about the question of soul fragments being old in one time-zone and young in another. If all time exists simultaneously surely a young soul or psyche, as you say, can also gain access to its older fragments and pick up knowledge without having to bother with the hard learning process?

ANSWER: One of the gifts of cosmic maturity is the ability of the psyche to draw knowledge and information from its other fragments, which only comes with the understanding and comprehension of Outer Time. Young psyches automatically think in linear time and it is not until they reach more advanced or broader states of cosmic awareness that their perspective affords them this reality. In acquiring wisdom they also become aware of the experiences of their other fragments and how to contact them. In the Paschat and Ishnaan cultures time concepts had long been taught to all. Although the principles were explained and accepted there were times when our planets did host those who were not sufficiently advanced to make inter-time contacts with their other fragments. Knowledge of a principle does not in itself necessarily endow one with the ability to utilize it at will.

QUESTION: You say we can experience in parallel timezones. Does this imply that we could be going through another life while we are living in the here and now and could this parallel life, for example, be in the same century?

ANSWER: But of course. Many of you are already aware of other existences in dream state. Parallel incarnations, linearly speaking, usually compensate your immediate life. I have helped Murry write a chapter about dreams to explain this as she has some fine examples at her fingertips; her own personal experiences, as well as information collected from tested and reliable sources that will serve as evidence for my statement.

QUESTION: Does creative imagination have any bearing on our development in Outer Time? For example, some people can visualize experiences in other galaxies quite easily while others cannot.

ANSWER: To develop creative imagination is a good thing for many reasons. It aids the expansion of consciousness which, in turn, helps you to grasp concepts a little beyond those to which you have been conditioned by the prevailing social and environmental trends. The ability to imagine creatively is not necessarily a hallmark of wisdom, as there are people who deliberately choose to block off past time experiences in your linear present in order to have a more peaceful life. There have also been instances where a mature essence-fragment has chosen to incarnate in order to introduce a new concept which is a halfway house to a future truth. Now that psyche, although subconsciously aware of the true facts, realizes that at that point in linear time your people are not yet ready to handle the complete picture. He or she is therefore obliged to effect a mental cut-off at a certain point which may cause much inner conflict. Such was the case with one of your great psychiatrists whose task it was to open doors, but only so far. However, because his inner knowledge was far ahead of the doctrines he expounded, and realizing that one step had to be taken at a time, he erected a mental barrier which produced psychological side effects.

To return to your question: an overactive imagination, if not properly controlled, can cause mental problems so care should always be taken in any meditative practices that may be conducive to wishful thinking.

COMMUNICATION

There are those amongst you whom you refer to as psychics, mediums or clairvoyants; even your most hardened cynics may visit such people. In fact, we have often observed members of your official medical and scientific bodies approaching this or that psychic secretly for fear of ridicule from their fellow colleagues who, unbeknown to them, are visiting another one down the road. Hypocrisy, of course! Rather like the doctor who remarked to you, Murry: "I don't believe in all that astrological superstitious stuff! But then I'm a Virgo and we're rational, clear thinking people, unlikely to be taken in by such nonsense!"

As the future has already happened it can be read by anyone with a degree of time consciousness, but there are pitfalls as we shall see. Good psychics can also scan time-zones in parallel universes, so they could equally pick up an experience you have undergone in your sleep state, or a secret wish. We intend to give you a few tips on mental time travel, but it might be advisable at this point to sort out the subtle differences between clairvoyance, astral projection, time travel, and the hypnotic state.

When practising astral projection an aspect of your psyche departs from its physical vehicle. You may find yourself able to move across the room, observe your body recumbent upon its chair, or even, pass through walls, because this subtle essence functions at a different frequency to its physical counterpart and is not, therefore, imprisoned by matter in this time-zone. In this form of astral projection you are limited, to a degree, to the time sphere in which your physical body operates. You may read of people who are able to project to Australia to witness the death of a much-loved relative, only to hear the following day that such a passing had in fact occurred. Bilocation can also be said to function in this manner, but how many of you have astrally projected in the way just described to the reign of Elizabeth I, or to the time of the

51

saurians? The reason for this is that there is a different principle involved, as we shall explain.

What about clairvoyance? Surely, you will argue, this is a form of time travel, for there are psychics who can see what your other fragments are doing and contact intelligences from times ahead of your own? Not necessarily! One can be aware of other time-zones without actually projecting to them either mentally or astrally. A psychic may tell you: "I can see you a year hence in a sunny clime," and sure enough, this prediction comes true exactly as described. Was that just a lucky guess? And, if not, from where did they obtain this information?

What usually occurs in such a case is that the psychic tunes into the subconscious mind of the enquirer via the right hemisphere of his or her own brain: in other words, telepathizes. A mental picture is then constructed from the impulses exchanged that will vary in detail and accuracy according to the state of health, mental perception and general well-being of the medium. The extent of detail brought through to the present will be reliant upon one rather important factor: the subconscious cooperation of the enquirer, as we shall shortly observe.

Another variation of this theme is where a strong desire or wish is transmitted from the querent to the psychic who simply returns what is being sent out and never makes contact with Outer Time at all. Let us use an analogy.

You turn on your television set and you see a picture. But if your set is not properly tuned you may receive it with distortions in sound and colour. The general idea might be correct, but the finer details inaccurate. The television set represents that part of the psychic's mind that reaches into Outer Time. Perhaps it has sustained a recent breakdown and is not functioning too well, or the channels have become crossed and the knob that reads Channel 3 is in fact picking up Channel 1. Physical or emotional stress involving either the reader or the enquirer will tend to produce a jagged or distorted set of translations, or there could be a breakdown in transmission so that the fault lies with the television station itself and not the receiving set.

Those of us who communicate across the barriers of time also have our problems and we can experience interference from many quarters, such as mental opposition from those on your own planet, or negative, incompatible frequencies from alien intelligence's. So there are several factors to take into consideration when assessing the reliability of channelled communications or psychic sight of any kind and, assuming that the message is received with a reasonable degree of accuracy, there is always the subconscious mind's private monitoring system to contend with.

A psychic who scans history for other lives is simply employing that aspect of his or her mental economy that can negotiate time curves. But because most of you are conditioned to linear time the tendency is to relate the experiences of other fragments of the essence to past eras on your planet when, in fact, no lives are really past, present or future, as we have already explained. This accounts for what must appear to you as anomalies in timing when incarnations appear to overlap. Of course, they can overlap, because we are dealing with Outer and not Inner Time. When you all eventually learn to time travel you will be able to discard intermediaries and move directly into those cosmic currents where events are actually taking place. But, as many of you will probably gather, it will take a great deal of mental discipline to handle this kind of realization and remain reasonably rational. So this has to be part of your linear future, by which time a generation or so will have been well programmed into the concept.

The human brain is similar to a computer and computers work on programmed impulses. In what you call 'trance mediumship' impulses transmitted by an external intelligence are relayed to the mind of the psychic where they are cerebrally decoded into terms appropriate to those for whom the message is intended. Distortions can occur for a number of reasons: a limited vocabulary, a lack of terms of reference available in the language, academic or intellectual limitations of the medium, or a lack of genuine knowledge on the part of the communicator.

For example, it is very difficult to pass scientific information through the mind of a person who has not been schooled in that discipline or who is incapable of creative visualization. The latter is most important as there are some people who, although they are trained scientists, do not have the capability for thinking beyond their text books or translating scientific principles either verbally or pictorially into terms easily understood by the layman.

A person with good visualization is of far more use to a communicating intelligence than a qualified person with a closed mind who is unable to correlate his or her ideas and discoveries to similar principles in, say, psychology, medicine, sociology or even philosophy. No doubt many of you will argue that if the time is right the information will filter through. That may be, but we can assure you that a great deal of mental effort often goes into getting things through on time – your linear time! I will leave you to work out that one for yourselves, but there is a logical answer if you care to think about it.

Your people have been searching in other dimensions for centuries, always knowing that there was more to be tapped but lacking the wherewithal to tap it. When the time is right a discovery or realization will occur simultaneously in several places on your planet: some call it the 'Law of Synchronicity'. A gentleman in Japan, a lady in Norway, a team working in Italy, and a doctor in Britain may all hit upon a similar idea around the same time. When the general evolutionary level of a planet is ready to take a step upwards, or in our parlance 'imbibe an understanding of another time-zone', a series of impulses is set into motion that interact with the group or collective thinking patterns, and the chrysalis makes yet another thrust in its laboured but purposeful effort to slough the skin of ignorance.

Where then, you may ask, does free will enter into this picture? There is a master plan or time map across which your essence has chosen to shed its fragments; each fragment being drawn to the individual blueprint appropriate to the time-zone in which it has elected to experience. Whether that blueprint is adhered to or not will depend on the free will of the essence as a whole, but there is no set time limit in the sense that you would understand it in linear time. If regression from the elected path does take place at some point in time, only the one who regresses is the ultimate sufferer, as we will explain to you later.

Any form of time-probe is beset with pitfalls, many of which can, if not correctly understood, cause upsets in your lives either as a result of distortion or apathy. A psychic reader may present you with a picture of your future that does not meet with your approval. "What a load of rubbish!" you may say, and you might well be right. Here is why. How much you or anyone sees of your future is usually dictated by your own subconscious mind which may release at any one time only the knowledge it deems necessary for you to have, so that you can negotiate a given situation or difficulty without altering any major decisions that constitute part of your karmic blueprint in the years ahead. In other words, do not rely on a reader to tell you exactly how to decide this or that, and do not expect to get that same information through hypnosis unless it is part of the designated plan of your life.

For example, were you to project forward, see yourself running a ranch in California, and then wait complacently for someone to knock on your door and give it to you on a plate, you probably would make no effort at all to achieve it. What is more likely is that you will receive an unsatisfactory answer either from a psychic or from probing your own subconscious. This will cause you to be thoroughly resentful about your whole situation to the extent that you pull up your roots and emigrate to America to escape from it all. A series of events then unfold after you have settled in your new land – events which ultimately lead you to that ranch in California. But these will have occurred as a direct result of your personal decision and not a 'cloud nine' promise made by some psychic practitioner anxious to please you and collect a fee into the bargain. Were you to be given too many details you would simply not take the steps necessary for life's next achievement, although the psyche does occasionally use the subconscious to supply the proverbial carrot that encourages the donkey to move forward!

Many of you will have encountered the type of person who regularly visits readers to ask the same question: "Am I going to win some money?"

The first psychic scans her tarot spread, shakes her head and replies: "I can't say I see a lot of money, dear, but there is a move across the water for you within a six."

"But I don't want to go abroad," the enquirer protests. "I want to win the lottery. Oh, to hell ....!" And on he goes to the next consultant.

"Mr. X, can you see me winning some money?" Mr. X consults his astrological charts and replies, "Not really, but there is a communication coming to you shortly which is connected with overseas travel."

"These people are all hopeless," our persistent enquirer complains in exasperation. "I can't get any sense out of any of them. All fakes! I'm packing up and getting away from this whole scene."

Mind you, the fact that a few weeks later a letter does arrive from abroad to tell him about a new job which he decides to take, and that the whole family embarks on the 6th of October conveniently escapes his memory. Years later, after having made a fortune sheep farming in Australia, he is sitting in retirement quietly watching the sun go down, when along comes his daughter with a new psychic she has just met in town. After introductions are effected, the clairvoyant looks closely at our friend and exclaims:

"Mr. B, there are not many occasions in my life when I've been able to tell anyone this, but I can actually see you winning a large sum of money!"

"Balderdash," comes his reply, but sure enough he wins.

The moral of this story is this: had that man been told years earlier of his win late in life he might have sat back and never achieved any of the things he did, all of which were important to the expression of his karmic blueprint.

Many of you who read this book will follow our suggested exercises and learn to negotiate time, but if you expect to see exactly what you will be doing ten or twenty years in the future you will be in for a surprise, for your subconscious mind will only allow you to filter back impersonal scenes that will in no way influence your decisions in the present. Hypnotists using progression are often faced with statements from their clients that make no sense. In these cases there are two factors to consider: the subconscious monitoring we have already discussed, and the intrusion of conscious rationalization.

Your famous prophets, such as the Brahan Seer and Nostradamus, were able to time travel, while Thomas the Rhymer actually admitted that he had been about the universe a bit in his time. But because the ordinary folk of those days had not been conditioned to the concept of other planets being occupied on any level his lengthy absences were attributed to excursions to 'fairyland' where the resident Queen Mab did him well!

Of course, many of these old prophecies were written in obscure terminology that could be made to fit several later developments. But as few people took much note of them, and those who did were in no position to alter the direction of events, it cannot be said that there was any real interference. But Nostradamus was from the future and he had seen it all happen already!

There is an erroneous impression held by many of you who consider yourselves to be enlightened that all good things come from your linear past. We are amused when we hear your people saying: "This was written in 1640, therefore it must be good." But when it is suggested to them that a different interpretation emanated from around 3500 BC that seems just a little too old to buy. Rest assured, dear things, Earth age does not guarantee truth and there are just as many good prophets alive on your planet today as there were in the Old Testament times of your Bible, or any period, in fact, that you care to name in your history.

We also observe a mistaken belief amongst you that the new generation of your young people are more spiritually advanced than their elders. This is not necessarily the case. Each generation has its own advance guard and the fact that your youth have been programmed to broader scientific concepts than their elders is not a valid criterion for their spiritual maturity. The lack of personal discipline among many of them is hardly the hallmark of a mature psyche. The cosmos, being an orderly affair, is not anarchistic and the seasoned time traveller, being well aware of this, will avoid the paths of abuse of the body, anarchy, revolution, hatred and bitterness. If you want to identify time travelled intelligences in any age group look for such qualities as absence of any kind of fanaticism, open-mindedness, compassion, tolerance, gentleness, caring, tenderness, non-aggressive questioning, sensitivity to all living things and, of course, love.

****

QUESTION: Are space-time stories in the popular entertainment media inspired by beings such as yourselves?

ANSWER: Sometimes. We work in many ways and through many people. But there are also people who live among you in Earth bodies who are just as wise in the ways of time and space as we and who have come from equivalent time-zones to ours. Such people simply remember and write. Sometimes details are inaccurate because the correct terms of reference are non-existent in your language, but details do not really matter; it is the conveying of a principle that is important. Cosmic teachers such as ourselves use many channels for communication and are by no means limited to what you generally term 'spiritualist groups'.

The media is a double-edged sword, agreed, but then so is all energy. An image projected into the homes of millions of people can constitute a force for good or evil or, to use our terminology, cosmic flow or tension. People will decide for themselves which of these alternatives they will choose to follow. For example, they may emulate the violent anti-social type who attacks the elderly and the frail, or they may follow the example of kindly caring characters shown in other presentations. The responsibility lies, to an extent, with those who have chosen to serve humanity via the media. Perhaps they began full of good intentions, but were waylaid along the route. So instead of carrying out their original helpful programme, they found themselves projecting a life style that hinders rather than assists many viewers or listeners. Much of what you think of as bad in your world is not deliberate evil, but sins of omission or weakness. Some people are easily led into becoming tools for those energies that are intent upon pulling your planet off its course, although they certainly did not start out with that intention in mind and would probably be horrified if it were suggested to them that *they* were off course.

QUESTION: Can stray energy fields around our planet manifest as UFOs?

ANSWER: But of course! Much of the phenomena associated with UFOs could be classified under this category, although not all of it. Just as people in your past clothed their ideas of fairies in the fashions of their period, so do those among you today project visions of UFOs as you think they ought to be. Much of it most certainly is in the mind, but you should also remember that whatever can be visualized can also be. We seem to think that one of your ancient Greek sages said something about thought preceding matter, while your old adage "as above, so below" would also apply here.

QUESTION: On our planet we have a lot of problems that result from the differences of opinion as to the role of the sexes and the use or misuse of those functions normally associated with the sex drive. Some of our cultures favour a system of patriarchal dominance while others feel that the neglect of the feminine principle is the prime cause of much of our aggression. In most of our major religions 'god' is usually referred to as 'he', which is distressing to some of us. Now on your original planet, and on Ishna, have you experienced any such problems?

ANSWER: Not really. The Paschat concept of sexual union has always been different from your own even in our primitive days, being primarily associated with the procreation of the species and continuation of the race. Of course we derived satisfaction from it, but this diminished as more mental interests slowly took over our lives, causing the whole process to fall into a more <u>civilized</u> perspective by our standards. The Crystal People never had this problem for, unlike your own, as well as ours in our early evolutionary cycle, their procreation methods were mentally calculated and not governed by emotional or biological needs.

On our old planet we were more by way of being a matriarchal society, as the leader of our elders was always a female Paschat while our temporal chief was male. But the latter never acted without first obtaining advice from the former. Neither sex, however, was considered superior to the other. Only the age of the psyche mattered, and it was recognized that the leader of our elders always incarnated into female form specifically for that task.

The Crystal People are neither matriarchal nor patriarchal but absolutely equal in all matters. As they work on the twin system, each rank or position – be it spiritual or temporal – is always held by a pair. In this way they feel that the active and passive traits in both persons can blend together to create a balanced whole with neither dominating. It would be very difficult for you on Earth to tell the difference between male and female Crystal People as their genders are more of a spiritual and less of an obviously physical nature.

As for our concept of what you call 'god'. Well, as we have already explained, we see the Centre Point, or 'godhead', as an infinity of fully evolved and totally harmonious intelligences from every dimension throughout the universe, so how can it be either male or female?

59

HEALING

Your Earth at present could be likened to one of your hospitals in which the mental patients have tied up the doctors and taken over. Medical supplies and equipment are being experimented with by the mentally unstable, while the real sufferers lie unattended. But as certain subtle forces come into play on your planet, the genuine doctors will break loose from their bonds to heal the truly sick, all will gradually become calmer and order will be restored.

You may ask how this fits in with time? When an essence-fragment requires a particular kind of experience it will be drawn to that time-zone in which it is likely to encounter the circumstances conducive to offering it the right opportunities. This may well involve entry into a zone of Inner Time which functions at a dense or physical frequency, such as your planet. Earth offers a rather specialized type of experience that involves healing, and intelligences from, many other cosmic frequencies have actually homed-in to study and observe your therapeutic and correction techniques. Essence-fragments from other dimensions who have become out of balance with the cosmos are also drawn here and much of your present chaos results from there being too many patients and too few healers.

Many who are from time-zones far ahead of yours in Inner Time have also come to learn about suffering in order to understand the application and reception of healing. You may find it difficult to conceive of how anyone could actually wish to suffer. In Outer Time a lifetime of suffering is less than a microsecond and simply adds to the depth of vision of an evolving being. Sometimes there are those who will take on a difficult body, not because of what their other fragments have done in different time-zones, but to help those who will be responsible for caring for them to develop the love, dedication and understanding that will be necessary.

We Paschats sometimes come to your planet as members of the cat family, and from what may appear as an unintelligent observation post we have learned much of the human condition.

Notice how much a cat sleeps. In sleep state it travels into different time-zones, some of which are far ahead of your own both in terms of Inner Time and evolution. It is a fact that felines are great healers, especially of the human mind. Not all cats on your planet are cosmically mature, however, just as not all hominids are of the same time-age. However, as felines my kind can view your race and your problems dispassionately.

At this point I would like to introduce you to another member of the Paschat fraternity, my female companion, Mikili. Both Mikili and I have been tutored over many time-zones by a great cosmic Teacher who will be speaking with you later. Mikili's special interest is in healing, both physical and mental. You would probably refer to her as my wife, but among our people the relationship is more of a polarity or syzygy. Either way, she and I are very dear to each other.

****

MIKILI: I should like to offer some help and advice regarding healing, but the transition from your present attitude towards this study to a more effective understanding in the future must of necessity be a slow one, as I shall try to explain.

A healer does not really heal; Your healers are simply those whose psychological and spiritual make-up is of such a quality that energies are passed through them and are transmuted or transformed in such a way that they can easily be utilized or absorbed by others. Whether or not the recipients choose to accept those energies to help them heal themselves is another matter. Of course, I am not referring here to clinical healing such as the setting of bones, manipulation, surgery or those services that are offered at the more practical level, although even their successful outcome depends, to a degree, upon those subtle aforementioned energies that can be drawn directly from the cosmos by the patients themselves or channelled through those individuals you call healers. And, of course, the third factor to be taken into consideration is that of free will.

You may consult your doctor but receive no satisfaction, so in despair you turn to alternative therapies, such as acupuncture, naturopathy or radionics, and for a while you may feel better. In fact, quite a few minor ailments can be dealt with quite satisfactorily at this level, but as Inner Time creeps on the same problems recur time and time again. Why is this? It is because so many of your well intentioned healers are curing the effect and not the cause. Ultimately there is only one person who can cure the cause – and that is *you*.

Healers may pass energies to you and the wavelength of one healer may prove more compatible or easier for you to absorb than that of another. When healing is rejected, which frequently occurs, we hear such comments as: "It was not his or her karma to be healed." The truth is that the person who has the condition or imbalance alone holds the key to its cure.

"Not true at all," I can hear someone protesting. "After all, Mrs. X has been to every doctor and healer available; no-one could have done more. Besides, who in their right mind would choose to suffer like that?"

But that is where the mistake is made. Suffering *is* taken on by many of you and although your rational conscious mind makes valiant efforts to rid the body of this or that malaise, the subconscious stubbornly resists all external efforts to effect a cure.

So-called 'miracle cures' only occur when the subconscious mind programmes the body into accepting external help, and even then the results will not be permanent unless the *raison d'etre* is fully understood. In one of your major religions there is a reference to a man who was healed because his sins were forgiven, the inference being that the karma causing that disability had been assuaged, or he had subconsciously realized that it was no longer necessary for him to subject his physical body to a series of painful malfunctions in order to atone for wrong doings in another time-zone. In the case in question, energies flowed from one who was from Outer Time – or the future, as you would say – that were sufficiently penetrating to effect this enlightenment. But the lesson really being given was that the key to wholeness lay in understanding the cause which, in turn, provided the stimulus necessary to effect the transmutatory process that brought about the 'miracle'. Others could receive a similar energy flow but not respond in the same way.

If caught in the wrong time-zone a psyche will often choose to eject, causing much perplexity to those around it who have grown to love it. But perhaps it felt the need to return to where it really belonged. Your Victorians had a saying appropriate to this. When one of their children died they would often remark that he or she was "too good for this world." How near the mark they were!

Although the knowledge might come as a shock to some of you, many terminal illnesses are, in fact, death wishes carried out in what the psyche, via the subconscious, deems to be a respectable way to depart without causing embarrassment. The death syndrome is one of your great moral dilemmas. Until you can learn to pass graciously and peacefully from one time-zone to another by a voluntary action of will you will be plagued by those killer diseases which provide convenient exit doors.

In Inner Time you need a physical body as a vehicle through which to express yourselves, but in the time-zone following – that which you call 'death' – such a body is not essential, so it must be discarded. I see great fear amongst you concerning this transference of consciousness to the extent that many of you feel it necessary to effect early transitions through illness or accident. Were you simply to announce that you had learned enough and were ready to leave someone would be upset or hurt in a personal or selfish way, the economy of the family might be adversely affected, or the law of the land broken. When your society has sorted out its natural economics we trust you will be able to take your leave in accordance with Cosmic Law. Although there will always be the occasional accident or sudden departure, anxieties about contracting terminal diseases will be slowly lifted and, without resentment against life and its ills or blame being placed on anyone around you, you will feel free to make the decision to shed your present body. However, were you to act in this way as things are at present on your planet, few, if any, would understand and your medical profession would fight to stop it. Another factor to be taken into consideration is the existence of a certain unscrupulousness within your society that has to be eliminated before you can negotiate a stage of natural exit by will.

Later we would like to help you with some self-healing methods, but first there are points to be clarified. Healers may pass on energies until they drop from exhaustion and yet meet with no visible or tangible results, for if that patient is not ready to be healed, or has a mental resistance to wholeness, no change in his or her condition can occur. There might be some temporary relief resulting from sympathetic or kindly thoughts from the patient to the healer in appreciation for the help that is being given and, perhaps, to instil confidence in the healer's work, for many patients who consciously seek help but unconsciously reject it, and genuinely feel sorry for those who are trying to assist them.

Ultimately every person must find his or her own healing key, perhaps through experimentation or by employing some of the simple techniques we will pass on to you. In this way you will find your own karmic blueprint so that you can call upon the energies of many time-zones to help you to cope in your present Inner Time. When Earth enters its next evolutionary level you will not need a healing intermediary because you will learn to draw upon and master the necessary energies for yourselves. Alternative therapies afford a good bridge during the period of change through which your planet will be passing in the ensuing epoch, but ultimately there will be a technique which will involve returning sicknesses or difficulties to the time-zone in which they originated. This idea is not unfamiliar to some of your psychotherapists who firmly believe that disease-inducing traumas need to be relived before they and their somatic side effects can be finally expunged.

Chemical imbalances in the human system inevitably stem from some maladjustment in the psyche that is passed to the brain via the subconscious mind. Imbalances of this nature are often caused by severe shocks experienced in another time-zone, the effects being brought over from what you call the past. So as fast as your people gain mastery over one disease another raises its ugly head, this being because karmic imbalances *will* find outlets until you have learned to leave your former traumas in their timezone of origin and not project them into the present. But before you can achieve this you must learn about and fully comprehend the oneness of all time.

Because Earth is a planet out of its correct time sequence it has become a gathering ground for many time-lost intelligences in need of help. Certain of your esoteric schools already teach that yours is the planet of music and healing or replacement, although much of what is termed 'music' in your society today does little for the sick, of *that* we man assure you! Energies misused or misplaced have to be returned to their own position or replaced before the diseased fragment man assume wholeness. So if, for example, you bring through discordant energies from ancient Rome they must eventually be returned to that point or they will create an endless series of phobias, obsessions and fears. When, in the employment of hypnosis and some forms of psychoanalysis, the vital point is triggered an abreaction ensues and the therapist must ensure that his or her patient returns to fame that sequence until it is fully expunged both consciously and subconsciously. Likewise, time-healing will involve the sick person projecting to the time-zone in which the problem arose, facing it and leaving it there. In your modern esoteric parlance this is referred to as 'transcending karma'.

Many of your modern diseases have resulted from energies that have escaped from their correct time circuits, cancer being a typical example. Another future method of healing will involve changing the frequency to one which that disease cannot tolerate or exist in. A cancerous entity (such minor intelligences are present in all cellular malfunctions) mould not exist in our Paschat time-zone because conditions are neither ripe for nor conducive to its manifestation, let alone its growth. We have long since mastered techniques for engineering and controlling cell growth, as you will also do in the fullness of time.

I will now hand back to Kaini who wishes to add his comments to mine.

KAINI: Many of you who read this will have been taught healing techniques in the past, and Mikili has already told you what takes place when energies are transferred from you to your patient. Whether you believe these energies to come from a deceased Chinese doctor, a Red Indian medicine man, a Victorian surgeon, Jesus, or the planet Venus matters not. These are simply labels adopted by the conscious mind as terms of rational or religious reference to give both healer and patient a degree of confidence in the qualifications or sanctity of the source. Equally, healing energies can be transferred to you through your orthodox medical practitioners plying their trained profession, so do not simply dismiss this branch of healing out of hand. Many a surgeon or general practitioner may be every bit as skilled, if not more so, than those charismatic personalities that pack your meeting places and stimulate mass emotion through their demonstrations and orations.

Colour healing is another method that engenders faith in many of you, but in truth it works on the same principle as everything else. For example, red infers energy and warmth, while blues and greens are more of a cleansing and soothing nature. By projecting this or that colour, the healer is simply conveying the energy associated with its frequency which is, in turn, translated for utilization or rejection according to the will of the patient. In other words, it is effective as long as the patient accepts the healing and is subconsciously happy to retranslate the colours into the appropriate curative context.

At no point short of the Centre is intelligent life completely free of all imbalances; even a lack of full knowledge may constitute an imbalance at some point in time. If pressures are not of one sort they are of another. The diseases you have suffered through the evolutionary processes on your planet have been many, varied, and in accordance with the general progress (or lack thereof, as the case maybe) of Earth as a whole entity. Primitive people did not suffer from many of the same diseases that you do because, for one thing, their diet was different, while many of your people over the ages have lived under very unhygienic conditions, thus offering themselves as breeding grounds for various virulent strains of disease that have wiped them out by the thousands. Even today, most of your illnesses are caused by the way you mistreat your bodies: lack of hygiene, failure to understand and accept the true nature and role of certain bodily functions, incorrect eating habits, too much or too little fluid, too much protein, and alcohol and drug abuse. One could go on.

So you learn to keep yourselves clean, to stop smoking, not to overindulge in this or that, and to use your organs for what they were primarily designed, thereby eliminating a whole series of diseases that have plagued your peoples in the past. But the next onslaught takes the form of illnesses associated with the moral patterns of your accepted codes of behaviour, or by tensions generated by the demands of the age in which you live. You become tense because you are overworked; because nobody loves you (or so you think); because you feel unable to express yourself artistically; or because you have no emotional outlets. These tensions are thrown back onto the physical body which then goes out of gear and your doctors tell you the resulting aches, pains and discomforts are psychosomatic. A good ninety percent of all illness in your world falls into this category. It is part and parcel of the evolutionary cycle through which you are passing.

Throughout the process of evolution tensions exist in a degree appropriate to each time-zone. These tensions are part of the natural order of the universe and without them, whatever form they may take, you would have nothing to push against. It is the natural heritage of each essence-fragment to thrust forward in its ever pressing effort to return to its point of origin. The nature of these thrusts will naturally differ with each genus or species, so that which would prove tensive for one stream or impulse would cause no distress at all to another.

We are taught that at the Centre Point all tension ceases and all inward development turns outwards, because from this vantage point the whole universe can be viewed in all time frequencies. But until any of us reaches that Centre Point we are constantly pushing against this or that tension. This inner knowledge has given rise to a series of philosophies that have appeared under many headings down the ages: the concept of dualism, good and evil, darkness and light, Horus and Set, Baldur and Loki, Jesus and Satan. But this takes us into the realms of an entirely new subject which is to be discussed later.

****

QUESTION: You talk about self-healing and say you will teach us some techniques for this. You also say that in order to heal ourselves we will need to send our problems back to those time-zones in which they originated. It may take us a long time to learn all this, so will there be an interim period when healers could do it for us until we learn to master the technique?

ANSWER: As I have already explained, there are those amongst you who are already working along these lines, including some analysts whose studies have given them a broad concept of the range and frequency of the human species. I feel you are thinking that it would be dangerous for people to experiment alone to try to find what their other fragments are doing in order to heal themselves.

This is certainly true of many cases in your present, and indeed for some time to come; as I have indicated, not everyone on your planet will be able to handle the concept of time consciousness.

But there are always those whose task it is to prepare the way ahead. May we remind you that when the study you call psychology was first introduced there were many who condemned it out of hand as superstition and anti-religion. But over the years the established view has mellowed, and many mentally sick people have benefited from the ministrations of those who work in your psychiatric profession. Psychology has also helped to break down many of your outmoded attitudes, especially towards non-hominids and the eco-life of your planet generally.

But in the future (and the present, as far as those who are ready to imbibe this concept are concerned) the method will simply involve entering a state of Outer Time consciousness. By using the positive application of mind power, or a disciplined thought process, it will be possible for the individual to home into the particular problem spot, experience it momentarily and then, having understood its lesson, expunge it from the subconscious. In many cases detailed recall will not be necessary and the experience will simply leave you with a feeling of having shed a burden or learned a lesson. The enlightenment could even take the form of a new understanding of the problem or sickness, which in itself is therapeutic and will soon have a curative effect on the body.

We will give you a few techniques to work with, but not yet. First of all, you should thoroughly familiarize yourselves with the Outer Time concept' so that you feel secure with your Personal and God symbols. These are your safe conduct passes through uncharted time-zones, and without them you could encounter problems. Those who read this book and want to know more will then be ready for any techniques we may give in the future.

QUESTION: You say all time is one; and yet in Inner Time there would appear to be a linear pattern, as with people who take disabilities from one life to another. How do you explain this?

ANSWER: Time is relative, which means it is relative to the time-zone in which it operates. You live in a dimension where time is measured by the movements of your planet and the wear and tear the effect of the continual journey of matter through space has on your physical body. Do consider, dear things, you live on a permanently moving space vehicle which is in itself stress-inducing. When you undergo an experience that evokes considerable emotion, such as a horrendous death, severe fright, or great physical agony prior to making your exit from one timezone to another, the sheer power or energy generated by that emotion is etched deeply on the Inner Time point of departure and communicated to your other essence-fragments wherever they may be throughout timelessness.

Let us say you have exited as a result of a severe blow to the head. When one of your fragments re-enters linear time the trauma of that injury may be re-echoed in the ensuing experiences to manifest as severe headaches, epilepsy or some disorder relating to that part of the body. Equally, if you have inflicted suffering on others which involves a particular section of the human anatomy, *you* could end up with a condition that deprives *you* of the use of that organ, limb, or part of your nervous system. The reason for this is that traumatic experiences, as well as affecting those who actually undergo the suffering, also generate energies that radiate out to encompass those who have been the cause of that suffering or have added to it in some way. Hence the concept of karma. Sweeping statements of this kind may cause many of you to look askance at some poor person suffering from a physical defect and start wondering what he or she did to deserve it, but as we have emphasized throughout this book this may not necessarily be the case. We realize it is one of the hallmarks of your present evolutionary stage to try to pigeonhole everything, but believe me this *cannot* be done in Outer Time. The whole process of human experience is far too subtle and complex to be so generally categorized. Of course, where Inner Time is concerned lives do *appear* to proceed in ordered sequence, but this is purely an illusion and there comes a point when a certain degree of time awareness has been reached that this becomes obvious. It is rather like the music student having to learn the basic laws of harmony before he or she can break them and create a composition based on more sophisticated sound combinations. It is necessary to learn how to formulate ordered patterns before a disciplined control can be effected over abstract designs.

QUESTION: Do beings like yourselves have any control over material conditions here on Earth? For example, could you help any of us or our friends out of a difficult situation, such as an emotional, financial or practical problem?

ANSWER: Apart from outlining a broad philosophy that it would benefit you all to follow, we may not interfere in your affairs. What happens is this: prior to your psyche entering the present time-zone plans were made in Outer Time for this person to do this, that person to do that, this relative to render practical assistance, that friend to help careerwise, this associate to give financial support, that partner to afford emotional support; and you likewise to do the same for others. In some cases, however, once born into Inner Time people lag behind their Outer Time good intentions, especially when the going gets tough, so planned commitments are not always fulfilled. We can help inasmuch as we can send mental promptings to those who are holding matters up, and if this fails there are others of the group entity who will step in and act as substitutes so that the karmic blueprint can be followed.

Time does play a role here; plans made in Outer Time for Inner Time conditions may fail to work out exactly, so adjustments have to be made. The old tale of a second or last chance is sometimes true.

There is another reason why it is difficult for anyone looking at Inner Time from Outer Time to pinpoint exactly when an event will take place. Even when you are actually experiencing in Inner Time, as you are on Earth, you find it difficult to place dates accurately when attempting to look ahead, as any of your psychics will tell you.

But if you were to contact people from, say, five centuries ago in your Inner Time, could *you* give *them* the sort of details they would ask for? You might search your mind for historical instances given to you at school and come up with the exciting news that this monarch or that leader was due to be assassinated, but could you tell a farmer how many of his cattle would survive the winter, or whether his fifth child would be that much wanted son? Fortunately, we are a little more *au fait* with those we have agreed to help, for we have made it our business to be so. Also, we have the added advantage of having developed technical equipment capable of storing minute details of information that we can obtain by transmitting a mental impulse to a central source. But we have only collected data essential to our work so we cannot come up with irrelevant trivia, such as the winners of your many sporting events. You are slowly working along these lines yourselves and are already able to store records in a way that would not have been possible for you a few years back. Just wait another few hundred of your Earth years and you will no longer need the assistance of beings such as ourselves.

QUESTION: There are many people who are afraid of eternity or perpetual existence. The thought of going on forever horrifies them and they would rather think that at death all strife ceases and there is permanent oblivion. Have you an answer for these people?

ANSWER: That is easy. For them oblivion will come because they desire it to be so. But this is only a temporary illusion and eventually in Outer Time it will pass. They will awaken from their stupor and take up the threads of experience once more. But if it gives them peace of mind to believe their exit constitutes a total cessation of all consciousness, then fair enough: so it shall be! Because some people think in terms of an Earth-like existence with all its pains, weariness and suffering they long for total annihilation in death. When unencumbered by the body the psyche can function in a purely mental state, which means that whatever it thinks *is!* So while there are sweet dreams or oblivion for those who seek the long sleep one day, as even your scriptures tell you, the awakening inevitably will come.

GOOD AND EVIL

There are Cosmic Laws that function regardless of how you on Earth or the products of any other evolutionary impulses might feel about them. The universe is an orderly place in its infinity and therefore *not* by nature anarchistic. I am sorry to disappoint those of you who are looking for an excuse to give vent to your destructive or negative tensions. Just as the effect of combining certain chemicals can be guaranteed, so it is with Cosmic Laws which are constant throughout all zones of time.

Some time-zones run parallel while others are opposite, giving the appearance of cancelling each other out. The theory of the latter is not unknown to your scientists and there have been many speculative guesses regarding the possible existence of anti-matter and its effects. I would rather deal with the more technical aspects of this study in a later document, as we are at present concerning ourselves with the nature of evil and its metaphysical implications as they relate to the state of timelessness. But suffice it to say that time-warps are involved in those energy misplacements that you have lumped together under the devil's umbrella!

Undesirable force fields are built up by tensive energies that are set in motion by intelligences both in Inner and Outer Time which operate outside the wavebands of Cosmic Law. There are techniques for avoiding them that involve sidestepping or changing to a time-zone wherein they cannot operate or are negated by counter forces. For example, certain diseases that existed on your planet in previous times have been conquered in your modern world, so that the evil they represented in their time no longer poses a threat.

Evil is misplaced or misdirected energy that is out of its correct time sequence. But there are many forms of evil, and to simplify it in this way might well give you the idea that we are denying its existence. Far from it. Of course it exists, but only as *relative to time.* A cannibalistic primitive would appear barbarous in the light of the accepted codes of behaviour in your present day world, whereas a few thousand years hence your present usual generation will be seen as bloodthirsty, warring savages by the standard of ethics then attained.

Anything that transgresses Cosmic Law, meaning that which does not flow with its impulses, could be labelled 'evil'. Those who choose to run counter to the cosmic flow automatically set in motion a series of opposing energies that assume form as they gather momentum, eventually becoming a collective identity which feeds greedily on all that is around it. This misplaced force field can be utilized by intelligences that have chosen to abandon temporarily the ways of Light and Love. Thus what are broadly referred to as 'evil forces' assume personalities according to the religious or philosophical inclinations prevalent in the age in which they first manifested.

Were your society correctly orientated time-wise much of what is generally referred to as evil in your world would not exist. Of course, there would always be those tensions that are part and parcel of the experience offered in each time-zone which usually result from the group or collective thinking of the race or planet in question. This concept has given rise to what you call dualism, or the idea that the forces of good and evil are in constant counterbalance. In one sense this is a fair assessment, for each time-zone does present relative tensions against which those functioning within that circuit can push or thrust. It is only when the accumulated potential of that tension mode becomes out of hand or out of balance that the resulting force field lends itself for utilization by energies incompatible with Cosmic Law. The troubles then commence, as with your Earth.

Certain errant energies can only operate within a given wave band; poltergeist phenomena for example, which results from an involuntary release of undisciplined psychokinetic energy. Misplaced or misdirected energy is by its very nature destructive, unless it is negated by its opposing force or anti-zone. There is an anti-zone for everything and we Paschats and our Crystal friends learned to negate incompatible energy fields, initially with sensitive deflective instruments and later by the use of pure mind power. The latter method entails mentally projecting the wayward energies into their appropriate anti-zone, or in the case of genuinely lost essence-fragments, returning the psyche in question to where it really belongs. Some of your occultists have already discovered how to inhibit phenomena in a similar manner and help rehabilitate lost fragments, these being the first stages in the technique.

Sometimes a fragment encounters tensions it feels unable to master so it chooses to avoid the issue, and in so doing appears to slide backwards or regress. This causes it to turn against the forward directional tides of Cosmic Law and, as like attracts like, when several such souls come together an 'evil' pocket of energy starts to coalesce. As they regress they drag others of their group with them and a spiral is formed that turns in on itself. I have heard your metaphysicians say that evil feeds upon negative thought and sometimes you give this evil force a name, such as Lucifer, Ahriman or Set, depending upon your persuasion. What is actually taking place is that the group concerned is pulling away from the Centre. Since all positive, constructive power emanates from the creative source, evil collectives find it necessary to swell their ranks in order to survive. They derive their sustenance from the negative energies generated by such things as wars, riots, violent crimes, mass discontent, oppression, or religious, social or political fanaticism. But, in spite of this, realization will eventually dawn and slowly the lost ones will abandon the false security of the negative grouping and return to the pathways of Cosmic Law.

Certain alien tensive force-fields are created by those beings from other time-zones who have regressed. Such beings as these you refer to as 'evil ones', and there are stories illustrating their fall from light, or regression from the Centre Point, in many of your religious teachings. It is always a 'bright one' who falls, you are told, but there are still many superstitious people amongst you who see these 'fallen ones' as demons of great physical ugliness. These are simply the fantasies of your own minds; you have clothed those negatively destructive energies in the guises you think fit them. Were you really to behold a regressed being, such as the one described in your Bible, you would be in for quite a shock for you would certainly not recognize it. Besides, it is always worth bearing in mind that in Outer Time there are no fallen beings in the way that you would conceive of them, for as all time is one your devils have long since taken 'U' turns and made tracks centrewards. Only you keep the memory of their misdeeds alive, thus perpetuating a fear and feeding personae that need never exist.

Pockets of misplaced energy can either be generated by intelligent thought, or through some evolutionary quirk in nature. It is always well to remember, however, that *good constructs* and *evil destroys*. A naturally destructive person is often out of his or her correct time-zone, although of course it depends on the context of the destruction. Allow me to elaborate.

Sometimes it becomes necessary to demolish in order to rebuild. When one time-zone is in the process of giving way to another this will tend to occur, as with your planet today and over the next one hundred years. Demolition of this kind is usually brought about by several contributory factors: the elemental kingdoms, animal group entities, external cosmic forces and, of course, decisions of war made by your own peoples. In a mass about turn, such as you will be experiencing on your planet during the Aquarian Age, both spiritual and somatic mutations will occur.

Matter can alter in shape and purpose and, likewise, the psyche can change direction. But, of course, this is not the end that your eschatologically-minded friends would have you believe, for life will go on. There have been instances in some galaxies where suns have collapsed, celestial bodies have collided and conditions conducive to life, at one level anyway, have been drastically changed, if not completely obliterated, but life has returned, albeit in a mutated, reconstructed or elevated form. Like the phoenix, a new race rises from the ashes of the old with a new understanding, a new lifestyle, and a new dimension of time consciousness. When one of your youthful progeny grows out of its clothing that apparel is discarded. To discard your physical body naturally at time of death or exit is not destructive as long as the intention behind this discarding is pure and in accordance with Cosmic Law. But if this process is hastened by one of your kind wishing to acquire the worldly goods of another, the intention has designated that passing to be a destructive or evil act, and the karma initiated between the people concerned would need to be played out. While it may be argued that all things that are destroyed are reabsorbed into the cosmos for recycling, there is also an ethic involved.

All must constantly change, but this does not mean that you are being constructive if you conveniently rid yourself of somebody who is proving a nuisance to you. All discarding must be a voluntary act of free will on the part of the psyche that wishes to exit. As the majority of you are still highly insensitive to many other forms of consciousness on your planet you tend to go about your path of destruction totally unaware of what you are destroying or the pain you are causing. But all that will end with time and the growth of your true sensitivity.

There is also a rather erroneous concept nurtured possessively by many of your occult traditions that all things evolve one into another. Throughout infinity each impulse evolves within its own kind. Paschats do not evolve into hominids, plant spirits do not become horses, nor gnomes become domestic animals. Each life stream is unique unto itself right to the Centre Point, where all blends into perfect harmony and each partakes of a full knowledge and understanding of all others. Of course, much of that understanding is picked up along the highways and byways of time. Such is the established rule. And yet within this infinite universe there must always be the possibility of exception. Certain intelligences or essences that are near to the Centre Point, such as those who have chosen the teaching role, are able to move into evolutionary streams other than the one in which they originated.

There is one other impulse or group entity to which this also applies. These are the Guardians of Cosmic Law who have the adaptability necessary to enter any time-zone or evolutionary frequency should the necessity to do so arise during the course of their duties. The name by which these beings are known to us would mean nothing to you, but as I know your predilection for labels I shall borrow a term from your religious orthodoxy and call them 'Seraphim'. But cases such as I have just mentioned are extremely rare outside of the cosmic teaching or policing professions!

I have often heard your people remark that the world would be a better place if everyone thought alike. But unison and harmony are not synonymous; unison implies a group entity or collective the members of which have not yet individuated. In order for the psyche to mature it is essential that it be afforded the freedom to express itself uniquely but harmoniously, in the way that a great orchestra produces beautifully blended sounds, with each instrument contributing a different melody or counterpoint. One jarring note, however, causes discord.

And so it is with your people. The process of cosmic individuation from the group entity calls for the retention of unique individuality on the one hand, while simultaneously blending with both younger and older psyches on the other. Notice two master musicians working together when neither tries to outdo the other; the result is a perfect blend of instruments or voices.

Having conquered the influence of hostile energies and come to terms with the tensions generated within a given timezone, one fords oneself ready to view the next, and with that widening of consciousness a new and different group of problems are presented. Let us take an example in your world today. You may say: "Look at the evil in our governments; nations war one against another; our leaders are unscrupulous, money grabbing ego-trippers; cruelty and fear abound at every crossroad. If this mess were all cleaned up we would have happy, peaceful lives."

All right, so the force of time does its work or, if you prefer, your Earth passes through or along one of time's corridors and emerges at the other end into a Utopian world where leaders are chosen for their spiritual maturity and not their bank balances or television ratings, where wars have been abolished, the lion lies with the lamb, and all nations co-exist in accord. But during the process of this transmutation, you have also advanced scientifically to negotiate time-zones beyond your own and move through space using newly discovered forces, or the type of energy we Paschats used to feed into crystals and carry with us while timetravelling during our early space pioneering days. Your next set of problems will therefore be interstellar ones, for you will no doubt have realized by now that the physical or interdimensional universes beyond your Earth are neither perfect nor trouble-free.

No doubt I will be taken to task by my Teacher for talking in terms of events so far ahead, when many of you feel the need for help to act against prevailing evil forces or misplaced cosmic energies that are troubling you in the present. There is no quick recipe for dissolving the tensions immediately surrounding your planet; this can only be achieved by a joint effort from all its life forms, plus a bit of encouragement from those such as ourselves who are not affected by it. What we can and will do is to give you a few 'safety first' rules for time travelling and avoiding the 'pasties'; the rest is up to you.

As we have so often said, like attracts like and purity and innocence are in themselves protections. But so also is knowledge, if rightly used and accompanied by wisdom. Fear, not to be confused with wise caution, is your greatest enemy and, strangely enough, it is one of your own creation. Dispel this and you will be well on your way to mastering your next time-zone and sidestepping those negative energy forms that are having a final fling at your expense.

****

QUESTION: You say we do not evolve from stones to animals and thence to *Homo sapiens,* and yet this is a teaching adhered to by many occult and metaphysical traditions. Why is this?

ANSWER: Each planet that houses life offers many different levels of experience to different genotypes. On your planet the dominant species is *Homo sapiens;* the essences of animals, plants and minerals are experiencing in less mature modes. Many of you are totally unaware of this, or the fact that on planets such as ours and that of the Ishnaans, the dominant life forms are different again. I can also assure you that there are worlds where forms of plant life are more highly evolved than yourselves in technological achievement and spiritual understanding. Your major religions are, unfortunately, responsible for your egodominance, which is a great shame, as it will come as a severe shock to many when scientific discoveries eventually disclose the true facts.

We also find it strange that you consider yourselves to be created in the image of the Centre Point which, in fact, has no material image and, if it did, each genotype throughout the universe would probably think of it as looking like itself.

WHY ME?

So often we hear it asked: "Why has this happened to *me?* Why was *I* picked out to suffer this or that? After all, Mrs. X and her family haven't had it! Why did *my* father die when I was born? Why do *I* have to be so poor?"

We observed one young lady on your planet seething with indignation when her child was born with a deformity which resulted from her frequent use of an hallucinogenic drug. "Why did God allow this to happen to me?" she wailed.

'God' neither allowed nor disallowed. She did it herself; no-one forced her to experiment with drugs. She could have said 'no', but she did not, and as a result her child will grow up in the knowledge that he could have been born whole if only…

No-one chooses, picks on, forces, decides, or sits in judgment of you!

Prior to entering into any one life the essence-fragment or psyche in question chooses a rough blueprint for that existence. This choice will be based on the overall pattern of what you refer to as your karma, or the particular time-route by which your essence has elected to travel on its return journey to its creative source. Youthful fragments often do not possess the wisdom to make clear choices and are therefore drawn into those streams of consciousness that are likely to accommodate their desire nature, like attracting like. More mature fragments, having learned discernment, are able to effect a wiser selection.

The permutations of time experience are infinite. You can negotiate any number of time routes and may often appear to double back on yourself, but eventually you will reunite with the other fragments of your essence and return to the Centre Point. Time travelling must and will vary with each individual, but should you choose too go against the flow of Cosmic Law and pursue a path of 'evil' your journey will, in the long run, be a much more painful one.

Let us return for one moment to healing. Bearing in mind my comments about tension in each time-zone, why should this tension manifest as one type of illness in one person and another type in the next? Or why does the pace of life leave Mr. X with a heart condition, or Miss Y with renal problems, while Mrs. M keeps perfectly fit? As we have already established, traumatic experiences leave scars on the psyche; if you rub a scar it will become sore sooner than an area of healthy tissue. Create a tension in a balloon by over-filling it with air and it will burst at the point of weakness. Here are some examples of how your psyche can become scarred; why one person has a phobia, another suffers from lung troubles, and another is overly sensitive to cold.

Suppose your problem is of a psychological nature and you seek the services of a psychotherapist who uncovers the fact that you have nightmares about tigers because you were killed by one while out hunting in Bengal with the Raj in the last century. Naughty, naughty! Tigers did not evolve on your planet to afford you or anyone else the pleasure of taking pot shots at them. Can you learn from this and overcome your fear?

Or perhaps you are frightened of the sea and during hypnosis the fact surfaces from your subconscious that one of your fragments became involved in a sailor's brawl after a drunken orgy, during which your mates appropriated your gold earring and threw you overboard to drown. Has that experience taught you not to mistreat your body?

Or perhaps it emerged that as an infant you were left outside, exposed to die by a family whose religion did not favour girl children; or that in another period you commanded an army which laid seige to that very township, causing thousands to die of cold and hunger. Have your learned from that experience?

Why Me? you ask. You, because *you* did it and no-one else, that is why! It does not really pay to go against Cosmic Law for ultimately you end up punishing yourself each time you do – a very good and logical reason for not pursuing the path of evil. "As you sow, so shall you reap," one of your holy books teaches. Being bad might seem like fun until you come to reap the cost and end up bemoaning your fate and cursing some non-existent entity instead of blaming yourself for your own plight.

Can any of these things really be corrected? Will burying your problems in the past restore an arm or a leg, or replace a surgically removed kidney? Of course it will not! But it will *help,* inasmuch as an acceptance of a situation can bring peace of mind which lessens the pressure on the weaker point. Acceptance encourages understanding, and to understand a problem is half the battle. So you only have one arm and others around you have two; many people have achieved great things with no arms at all and not resentfully buried their talent. Learn your lesson well and in another time-zone you will experience the joy of being fully whole. Enigmatical? Yes, but only if you view time as linear. Just telling sick people they are suffering because they committed this or that atrocity in another time-zone does not really help, however. Unless the lesson is subconsciously understood they will not respond to suggestions that they might conceivably have attracted the condition as a result of this or that behaviour. Also, the problem might not necessarily stem from inter-time karma at all, but from a desire to help others to understand and learn, as we have previously explained.

Come to terms with the fact that your bodies are not perfect; the reason for these imperfections can be traced to the way previous generations of Earth people have mistreated them. In future time-zones there will be no need for any of you to die after months of agony from some dreaded terminal disease; this is one fear from which you will be freed. But in return you will have to face up to the act of voluntary transition from the Inner Time of frozen energy to an Outer Time dimension of pure mind or thought.

Try to look after those little physical imbalances that may afflict you. You have a saying that 'cracked crocks last the longest', so there is no need to throw up your hands in horror at the first sign of wear and tear in your suit of bodily clothes. We have heard a person make the boastful statement: "I am as fit as a fiddle, never get a thing wrong with me. I eat and drink what I want, and smoke two packs a day and I've been well all my life!"

Oh dear, that poor soul will feel it doubly when his time comes. If he is fortunate enough to avoid sickness for a long period it will be only because time has not yet pushed the appropriate button.

In other words, his weak point or physical deficiency has not yet become apparent. But it will and then he'll wonder: "But why *me?*" Any abuse of the physical body will, of course, speed up the process of deterioration, so the choice is yours.

Another unfortunate person may have a weakness that manifests in early childhood and causes him or her to become the subject of cruelty and derision, but that same person may still be going strong when his or her tormentors have long dropped away. Those who realize their deficiencies in early life are often able to take extra care, wrap up warmly, eat sensibly, rest sufficiently, and last the course. Very good health in youth is often the hallmark of the younger psyche whose subconscious mind is blocked off from the wonder of Outer Time and all that that implies. When bad health does hit such people they are confused and bewildered, and it seldom occurs to them to turn to their fellow humans who have been suffering for many years and say: "Now I know what you have been through and I am indeed fortunate to have escaped it for so long." Such a statement *would* come, however, from a seasoned time traveller who is more cosmically mature.

Some of you who are experienced as healers will have noted that it is often much easier to heal animals that humans. Is there a reason for this? Yes. Animals, not being of the same cosmic impulse as *Homo sapiens,* are not subject to the human condition. But, like yourselves, all animals are not of equal evolution either spiritually or somatically, and many of them are more spiritually mature than the people who think they own them. Because an animal does not communicate in your languages, bother itself with pages of complex mathematics, build machines, or make fires, the general feeling is that it is less evolved, childlike, or simple. Nothing could be further from the truth! How many of you are sufficiently in touch with the spirit of your planet to know when to vacate territories prior to Earth disturbances?

Animals work on a different evolutionary principle from people. Were it deemed that felines should be the dominant species on Earth, the whole development of your planet would have taken a different course. But because the *Homo sapiens* strain predominates animals have chosen to adopt a submissive role, leaving their true intelligence in another time-zone to be contacted during frequent bouts of sleeping, as with the domestic cat. Although an animal may also suffer from a terminal disease such as cancer, it usually understands why it has that condition, for animals also have their karmic blueprints. Although they may outwardly protest against certain veterinary ministrations, deep within they are grateful for the care, attention and easing of their pains. It should also be borne in mind that much of their suffering has been brought on by the treatment they have received at the hands of your people over the centuries. In their natural state, when their time comes to exit they slide inconspicuously away to abandon their little bodies in some dark wood or beneath some much loved tree. They know far more than humans in many, many ways. Even wild animals know when one of their kind is ready to go and will leave it alone to withdraw slowly and peacefully.

Man, on your planet, has fallen a long way behind in terms of Inner Time and has, in fact, two time-zones to catch up on. This deviation has resulted in the unnaturally aberrant evolutionary diversity which partitions those who are at present incarnate upon your Earth. Such a broad disparity in cosmic age is tragic for all concerned, being uncomfortable for the mature psyches, and jarring and frightening for the young ones.

When young incarnate fragments are faced with things they do not understand and cannot assimilate, they become uncomfortable and resentful. This has no bearing, incidentally, on your present life age. A time travelled fragment could be in a youthful body and an inexperienced psyche in an older one; or even, perhaps, in a position of worldly authority. Equally, the converse could apply. Incarnate mature fragments who have advanced beyond the present Earth conditions in other time-zones will *find* themselves ultrasensitive to issues that do not appear to trouble the average person.

All of you on Earth, and even Paschats and Crystal People, may tread many pathways to the Centre and during those time journeys similar signposts or metaphoric 'cosmic hostelries' could be encountered. The filth and degradation of one stopping place may appal you to the extent that you decide to give it a miss, camp in the clean open air under the stars, and drink the water from the fresh stream. The next traveller, however, may have other gratifications in mind, so the motives of the inmates of that tavern and the cleanliness of its night offerings are never questioned.

They sign in, are robbed of all they possess, catch a disease and become sick with sour wine and bad food. These are the hedonists who always suit themselves, putting their own comfort and pleasure above all else. They chose to stay at that hostelry because it promised them a good, comfortable and easy time. But, because they lost out as a result of their choice, they pass on to their next port of call, or stage of cosmic growth, resentful of being sullied by social diseases and robbed by unscrupulous rascals. So, in another time-zone they become extremists without quite realizing why, decrying anyone who ever looks at alcohol, persecuting those of easy virtue, or perhaps entering a strict religious order to the exclusion of all worldly conditions.

Yet the situation must arise when they will have to return to that point in cosmic time at which the wrong choice was made and once again be faced with the decision: "Shall I or shall I not stay at this inviting-looking hostelry, wherein I could doubtless have a good time, or shall I make for the green meadow beyond?" Maybe yet again they will take the wrong turning; or perhaps by then they will have understood the message, in which case the karmic wheel will stop turning and they will be free to enjoy more mature time-zones. The lesson lies in their being able to recognize the inn for what it really was and not be taken in by flashy externals or promises of comfort and physical satisfaction. When they can stand on that threshold and say: "But just a minute! This is a dirty place, the odours from it are foul, the vibrations bad, the leering faces of the inhabitants are cunning. No, I think I would prefer yonder meadow with the stars to light my bedchamber, the flowers as my companions and the waters of the pure stream to bathe my tired body and assuage my thirst." That would be a lesson learned and a time-link in the fetters of experience broken forever.

Time is always the answer. At some point or another all of us in the universe take a wrong turning which necessitates our relocating that crossroad once more and starting over again. Time – Outer Time especially – is the ultimate healer of all ills. Learn to come to terms with inter-time existence, close the gap between yourself and the Eternal Now and you will be well on your spiritual way.

****

QUESTION: You say that in order to expunge a trauma we need to return it to the time-zone in which it originated. But isn't this simply pushing it back into the subconscious and creating even greater frustrations?

ANSWER: No. Most of you are totally unaware of what is going on in your subconscious minds unless it is brought to the surface by some form of therapy, or through mental disciplines on your part. In order to expunge a time-trauma it is essential that it be brought into conscious awareness. By returning it to the zone of its origin you are doing just that, thereby freeing the subconscious of its burden. To become aware of your enemy is half the battle, I have heard some of you say. Even if you have difficulty in accepting this concept on a rational basis, the very fact that it has been brought to your notice is a help in itself. But complete freedom from its effects will not be achieved until a full understanding of its lesson has been grasped.

QUESTION: Do animals also incur karmic debts? Surely they are not all angels and must also make mistakes just as we do.

ANSWER: The animal kingdoms have to learn just as you do, and they too experience in many time-zones until they come to realize the positive qualities of the cosmic impulse from which their species generated. Young animal essence-fragments are often barbaric and cruel, as are their equivalents in the hominid impulse. A tiger must learn that people are not there for him to attack and eat, but by the time he has gained this realization he will, no doubt, be sitting by some comfortable domestic hearth enjoying a plate of fish and a saucer of milk. Or, perhaps, he may even be a Paschat!

QUESTION: You have previously told us that fragments of our essence are scattered throughout Inner Time, and while it is possible for the more mature of those to contact the younger ones, the reverse is not true. But if these fragments are scattered at the same time, why are they not all the same age? Why should a fragment be young in one time-zone and mature in another?

ANSWER: The fragments of the essence are distributed from a state of timelessness and not at the same time, which implies a linear point of reference. Until their eventual reunification at a given stage in their maturity their Inner Time experiences will predominate, thus giving the *appearance* of following in a progressive sequence or moving linearly. A fragment is accorded an 'age' because of Inner Time, and while each of you is mentally confined to that dimension you will continue to see it this way.

Evolving essences utilize both Inner and Outer Time in which to maturate, but while limited to the confines of Inner Time their fragments are subject to the rules and conditioning applicable to the time-zone in question. Youthful fragments interned in linear circuits are denied access to their more mature modes by their own total unawareness of the existence of an Outer Time.

Experience in Inner Time is essential to the learning process of the evolving essences from certain impulses who are unable to comprehend Outer Time until they have gained the breadth of vision that Inner Time experience will primarily afford them. On your own planet there are many psyches whose more mature fragments are distributed throughout other sections of the universe. There are also mature fragments of other essences who have undergone their cosmic youth in galaxies far removed from your own. Inner Time circuits by no means constitute the essence's entire education programme. The essence of those fragments that have freed themselves of linear constraints is able to assess its evolutionary progress in the light of the interdimensional experience provided by Outer Time. This assessment is referred to in some of your Earth religions as the 'Judgment'. You have a concept of a celestial courtroom presided over by a 'divine judge', but the ancient Egyptians wisely observed that it is your own time-consciousness, as personified by Thoth the Lord of Time, which is the real adjudicator.

Obviously, there is a lot more to this than I am able to explain to you at the moment, being limited by Murry's understanding and interpretation of the concept. But I will try to take you a little way ahead so that when the time-bubble does burst, as it will in the future, you will not find it so confusing. By all means stay with the concept of linear spiritual ageing if you find that easier to comprehend, but eventually you will see it in a different light.

THE TEACHER

I, Kaini, am also a student and for my learning I turn to my own beloved friend and teacher. His name? The name by which we know him would mean nothing to you, although there are those amongst you who do acknowledge his wisdom and know him by another name. Mikili and I have asked him if he will add a few words to our humble teaching efforts to aid you all through the difficult days of Inner Time that lie ahead. So, dear things, we lovingly hand over to him.

THE TEACHER: For many of you the pursuit of knowledge has become the all-important factor in your lives in modern society. You want to know the answers; you want to know how things tick; you want to dissolve permanently all links with what you feel to be outworn and outmoded ideas. These are all healthy traits, my friends, as long as you take into consideration the fact that knowledge is not synonymous with wisdom, and you would all fare far better both in your personal lives and in the cosmic scheme of things if you paid a little more heed to the acquisition of the latter.

In the excitement of a new age it is easy to be blinded by the bright lights of technological achievement to the extent that the propensity for individual development becomes totally obscured. For your own sakes, my friends, I beg you to give time and thought to deeper matters to help you to balance your scientific achievements with emotional stability and inner security; the suffering caused by such a neglect could be overwhelming.

As the moving tides of development open the floodgates of the human psyche with increasing rapidity, it is essential that you cultivate a cosmic space age philosophy upon which to anchor your minds during the time of troubled waters and changing tides that lie ahead; a safe harbour, if you like, from which to witness the seaward gales that will be blowing human consciousness hither and thither as the barriers of time and space expand ever outwards.

Throughout the ages of Inner Time on your planet you have been taught that there is one great principle emanating from the point where all time is eternity or timelessness. This is the principle of Love; may it be your guiding light through the searching days to come. You may translate this principle in many ways: as compassionate humanism; as tolerant religion; as caring and serving; but ultimately, be it in Inner or Outer Time, Love is selflessness, understanding and gentleness tempered with firmness.

"Oh, dear," I can hear some of you saying, "it's the same old message all over again, and this time we thought we were in for some exciting new information."

But it is not quite the same because the time is fast approaching in your evolutionary cycle when it will no longer be enough to sit about in a church, hospital or school and say, "I believe." A belief implies that which is accepted, but not really understood or proven. With new knowledge to come from your own scientists in the near future, and from sources external to your own zone of time, the statement *I Believe* will be replaced by *I Radiate*.

In other words, you who are able to grasp the concept of time-consciousness will find yourselves able to externalize from Inner Time and lift yourselves beyond the confines of turmoil on Earth into Outer Time, from which vantage point you will get a clearer view of what has been and what will be going on. Then you can relay it to those who will need some guiding star to follow during the days of doubt and bewilderment. Faith will give way to positive action.

The Love principle is very much concerned with the cosmic forces that flow in directional impulses between time-zones. When these waves of energy proceed in an uninterrupted and harmonious manner they convey the principle of Love from the Centre Point, or 'god' as you call it, and only when these channels become blocked by tensive thought structures that have become out of balance does that Love principle appear to be held back or not function at full power. One of the lessons the evolving spirit has to learn is how to unblock those points that are dammed up; this applies both in the individual and group development of a planet or solar system.

Taking into account the absence of limitation in Outer Time these things will all happen anyway, as they have already taken place in the Divine Consciousness. But, as far as those in Inner Time are concerned, they are still acting out their contributory roles.

In Outer Time the philosophy is basically one of seeing all things at whatever scale you wish to view them. For example, your Earth can appear in your mind's eye as no larger than a golf ball; thus you may place it and all concerned with it into a clearer perspective. At present you see it as a large sphere because you are relatively small in proportion to its physical dimensions, just as the microbes in your body see your brain as some giant 'god' with the power either to destroy them, or act as a protector caring for their general happiness and well-being. It is all a question of microcosm and macrocosm.

The next stage in *Homo sapiens* spiritual development will be to project beyond the limited environment of their own planet into Outer Time, from which vantage point the errors of their present ways will become overwhelmingly apparent. One of your well-known writers grasped the idea when his character, Alice, proclaimed to her persecutors: "Why, you're only a pack of cards!" Whereupon they all collapsed and she was freed. As you are gradually able to externalize your minds and view Earth from afar, you will slowly find that you can master those circumstances over which you appear to have no control at the moment. Time and space will become your allies, not your enemies. The child plays with the kite; the kite flies high but it is driven to and fro by the winds, causing the child to run this way and that to hold onto his toy. Man is no longer a child, my friends. He must learn to control his kite and to power it himself so that he is not the slave of the prevailing wind. In other words, he must stop allowing his life to be driven by the winds of circumstance. Such is the next stage in the philosophy of Outer Time.

Mankind is ready to learn to use his mind power more positively and not always to rely upon others to do it for him. This applies just as strongly to externals and intermediaries, such as myself and my Paschat friends. We would far rather approach you as equals than as Teachers, but over the centuries the tutorial role has, unfortunately, fallen our way. I say "unfortunately" not because we do not love to help, but because our class is mainly a remedial one that should be much further advanced than it is. Only when the human race has reached a fuller understanding of Outer Time will it be able to stand on its own spiritual feet (metaphorically speaking, of course, as someone is sure to say that in some zones of time 'feet', as you see them, might not exist). While limited in Inner Time mankind's perspective of the universe is time-bound and he cannot fully grasp the principles of Love and universality in their cosmic context. From Outer Time you will find that view much clearer and many things will begin to slot into place because time philosophy is nothing if not logical, even by your rather suspect standards of Earth logic.

Life cells, when viewed at close range through a microscope, appear as a chaotic jumble, but if you withdraw and readjust your instrument you will notice a perfect symmetry emerging. So it is with Outer Time. The further away from which you can view life, the more its purpose and pattern will become apparent to you and its anomalies will dissolve into understanding. So use any time techniques we give you with benevolence, kindness, hope and love. Do not transgress cosmic laws and your planet will slowly proceed towards assuming its rightful evolutionary time-place.

PASCHAT EXERCISES AND MEDITATIONS

A. PERSONAL AND GOD SYMBOLS

Your Personal Symbol:
Each and every individual has a symbol which is personal to him or her. It maybe some simple object such as a white flower, a yellow ribbon, a star form, an animal, a blade of grass – *anything* at all. Never dismiss an impression because it may seem too mundane, as all is permitted. It is quite possible that someone else may have a similar symbol to yours; this does not matter and simply indicates a group connection.

The Method:
Your last real contact with Outer Time, and therefore with your subconscious mind in its purest form free from environmental programming, was just prior to your conception, so this is what you do:

Seat yourself comfortably, or you may lie down if you wish. Close your eyes and take an imaginary journey backward through time to the moment of your birth. Enter the womb at the point of your actual conception just prior to when you made contact with the embryo that was to become you. Pause for one moment and then start to move forward in time, passing through your embryonic growth and the drama of your birth, and as you do so imagine that a silver cord extends from your baby-form. Take hold of it and pull it along with you as you proceed forward towards the present. Pass through the experiences of childhood, pausing here and there to register some particularly traumatic or meaningful event, great happiness, pain or new awareness, each time recording it by making a knot in your silver cord. Continue travelling mentally through your teenage years forward to whichever part of your life you have now reached, *but always imbibing the sensations of each incident and knotting your cord accordingly!*

At last you will arrive in present time trailing your knotted silver cord. Take the babyhood end of the cord and join it to the end which represents the present, thus creating a circle after the style of the ouroboros. This circle will represent the sum total of your Inner and Outer time experiences as related to the Now.

Continuing to use your creative imagination, lay the circle flat and step into the centre of it. You will immediately find yourself sinking fearlessly down through a gentle darkness. Gradually descending, you will eventually touch down. This experience will vary with each individual, but the bottom is often a muddy or watery base representing the primordial womb. Keep relaxed, breathe slowly and deeply; you will automatically start to rise again, but the way in which you rise will be unique to you! You may find yourself ascending a flight of stairs, flying with wings or climbing the side of a mountain, but whatever the method involved, you *will* ascend.

The first thing you see when you reach the top of your well or dark passage will be your own Personal Symbol. For example, you may find yourself plodding up a long flight of stairs and upon reaching the top you notice a window. Looking out of that window you may see a tree in full blossom; that tree will be your Personal Symbol. Or, instead of a window you may find a door which you open to reveal a hat hanging on a peg; that hat will be your symbol.

Until you try you won't know, but it *must* be the *first* impression that comes to you. No use trying again because you see a woolly lamb the first time, and being not particularly keen on sheep you have another go to see if you can get a silver cross which you'd much prefer. Perhaps the shepherd is your Archetype and the sooner you come to terms with yourself and stop chasing the hierophantic mode the better.

Having learned your true Personal Symbol, always keep it in mind for safety as it will link you with the energies of your group entity. Visualize it when going to sleep, when frightened or tired, or when effecting any form of time travel or altered states of consciousness.

Your God Symbol:
The next symbol you need to know is your God Symbol, which is your additional protection because it represents your own direct personal link with the Centre Point of the universe: God, the Ultimate, the Creator, the Is, or whatever you choose to call it. This symbol you may also share with others of the evolutionary stream or impulse from which you have originated.

The Method:
Having fully familiarized yourself with your own Personal Symbol, relax in a meditative posture and visualize it as strongly as you can. Enlarge the Symbol in your mind's eye until it becomes something in which you can sit. If it is a tree you may recline in its branches; if a swan, you may seat yourself on its back; if a star, you may sit astride its points, and so on. Feel absolutely secure in your hold, then proceed as follows: Start to rotate your symbol clockwise, slowly at first, but increase your speed as you spin.

Close your psychic eye so that you do not feel dizzy or giddy. You may find you need to give the whole process a little push to start with, although some people who have tried this have gained momentum with a minimum of mental effort. It does not matter how long it takes as this will vary with the individual. For a moment or two you will spin, and then you will slow down, come to a halt and land somewhere in Outer Time. With your mind's eye look around. The first thing you see will be an Archetype appropriate to you who will greet you or give you some point of reference.

For example, you may find yourself in a lush meadow where a lady wearing a blue gown and crowned with flowers comes forth to greet you. She may take the wreath of flowers from her head and present it to you; that wreath will be your God Symbol. Note also the nature of the Being who greets you. In your terms of reference it could be a god or goddess, a maternal or paternal figure, a personality associated with your particular religious faith, or a Cosmic Being. But whoever you see will represent the other half of your natural spiritual polarity.

One basic code that operates throughout the cosmos is the Law of Polarity. Every living thing must conform to this law which means that no matter how its consciousness may manifest, one or other polarity aspect will be dominant. This Law designates either the positive mode which manifests in an outgoing, active, directive, or Yang expression; or the negative mode which, when used in this context, simply implies the reflective, passive or receptive quality of the Yin, and *not* evil or misplaced thought or energies. Neither does it have any bearing on the gender into which you incarnate in any one particular life. The Law of Polarity is grossly misunderstood on your planet, as many who are incarnate in male bodies often experience difficulty in accepting the receptive/submissive mode. But rest assured that if you are able to come to terms with your true self, you will be much happier and more content.

The psychiatrist Carl Jung referred to the receptive or feminine as the *anima,* and the directive or masculine as the *animus.* Your ancient Greeks did a better job of unmasking these roles in the human psyche, however, so if you are in any doubt you would be advised to seek the appropriate clues in the Olympic Pantheon. [See *Practical Greek Magic.*]

Having now established your Personal Symbol and your God Symbol, may we reiterate that you should always use *both* when undertaking any form of psychic or occult work, time travel or meditation. These are your security codes and will ensure you safe passage through the unfamiliar territories of altered states of consciousness.

These two disciplines are specially designed for those who have no particular belief or religious adherence and they are every bit as efficacious, if not more so, than many of the so-termed 'safe passes' handed out by gurus or the more conventional religious, occult, or psychic organizations.

B: TIME PROJECTION AND PERSONAL DISCOVERY

You all have your fair share of worries, no-one is exempt from them. Let us say you are anxious about a house into which you wish to move, or how your child will fare at school in the forthcoming exams. You cannot control the outcome, yet you fear the worst. Or, it may be an emotional affair that is plaguing you and you seriously doubt whether the object of your affection returns your feelings. How can you survive without him or her? Will you ever be able to surmount this upset or that disappointment; this loss or that deprivation? Perhaps it is a health problem and you are concerned whether the operation will be successful, or if that strange nagging pain will go away of its own accord. "Make time your ally, not your enemy," we have stressed to you. But how? Here is a simple technique for helping to alleviate the tensions caused by a worrying situation in the Now. However, let us make one thing quite clear: *We cannot take your problems and concerns away from you, but we can show you how to use the faculty of time to help yourself through them!*

I will show you how to project forward using whichever of the two following techniques you find the easiest.

Method 1:
Relax and think of your problem; examine whatever it is you fear the most or the very worst that could happen. Visualize your Personal and God Symbols firmly in your mind. Start to imagine yourself swirling in a clockwise motion just as you did when you spun yourself around to find your God Symbol, but this time set your mental coordinates for a designated period into the future, say three years.

You will find yourself whirling faster and faster until you reach a moment of complete stillness. In that stillness you will be time travelling. There is no sensation of speed in Outer Time, only in the impetus of initial 'takeoff' and even this can be eliminated with practice. Having travelled forward in time you will then find yourself 'landing' somewhere three years hence. You may experience a series of mental pictures, but not necessarily so. If you do, however, relate them to your present day problems. For example, a cottage with a green door may be your own subconscious mind's way of telling you not to concern yourself about your present housing problem. Or you might gain the impression of having tea in amicable circumstances with a person whose motives you have recently questioned.

But more than likely your mind will simply blank or come to a halt, and when this occurs here is what to do. Imbibe the atmosphere and sensations that you feel in that future period, noting a completely different set of tensions from those worrying you in the Now. Also, your present problems will no longer exist for they will have been long resolved. Stay in your three year ahead time period for a moment or so, long enough to exchange today's worries for whatever tensive times may lie there, but because you have not yet reached that time-zone those worries relevant to it will have no importance and therefore produce no tensions for you in the Now.

Slowly imagine yourself returning to the present time. There will be no need to spin in order to achieve this; you will find it quite easy to return simply by thinking yourself back, but be sure that you are well earthed. [For safe earthing procedures see *Practical Techniques of Psychic Self-Defence.*]

When you finally open your eyes in the Now your present worries may still be with you, but your attitude towards them will have subtly changed because your subconsious mind has been reminded that all will work out and the sensations accompanying that relief will slowly filter through to your conscious mind. Try it. It really works, as Murry and her friends have discovered.

Let Time by your servant, not your master!

Your Personal Affinities.
Just as you each have a Personal Symbol, it is also possible for you to discover much more about yourselves as individuals through identifying your cosmic origin, element, animal, flower, tree, colour, number, stone, metal and musical note. How can this be done? My first suggestion was that armed with your Personal and God Symbols you spun into Outer Time. Well, here is another method that might suit some of you better.

Method 2:
Imagine the face of a large clock equipped not only with hands and hours, but also with years, like a giant calendar. In the centre of this timepiece is a series of dials you can set by adjusting them to the year to which you wish to travel. Seat yourself mentally on the face of your clock; having set your dials, press the 'forward' button and away you go. Your clock face will start to spin, taking you with it until it reaches a point of stillness. It will then slowly stop and the results will be exactly as with the former method. Those of you who have been thoroughly programmed into Inner Time may find the clock face method easier to work with.

In order to find the other personal associations mentioned, return to where you located your God Symbol – be it at your mother's knee, a seashore, a meadow, some distant galaxy, or whatever – and proceed from there.

For example, let us say that you contacted your Archetype in a flowering meadow and your God Symbol is a wreath of flowers. There you have your personal flower to start with and the colour of the flower will give you your personal colour. Look around for the presence of an elemental being in the form of a hobbit or gnome, fairy, ondine, sylph, or salamander. This will tell you the element predominant in your nature. Note the nearby tree, a shiny stone in the stream, a jewel lying on the grass, or whether there are any animals present. You may hear music and if you can hum the note or tune, try to remember it when you return to the present. Absorb everything quite slowly, a piece at a time. I will give you a table to fill in as the discovery of your real Self in Outer Time unfolds.

Your tendency on Earth is to form a protective shell or cover around yourself to hide your true nature under a false exterior of pride, fear, or just plain lack of confidence. So, in these discoveries you might well be in for a few shocks! But whatever the result of your quest might be, a better *you* will ultimately emerge from it and that will add up to happiness, peace of mind and inner security.

There are many other techniques I could teach you: form changing, self-healing and externalization, for example, but these are subjects for later lessons. I do not feel that you are quite far enough through the transition stage as yet to explore the cosmos unaided and unguided, so for the time being the aforementioned exercises and meditations will help you to take the next steps forward into Outer Time in safety and security.

Ultimately you will learn to heal yourselves, as Mikili and I have already explained, but we are limited to the capacity of the minds of those through whom we communicate, and enough is enough in terms of Inner Time. Information needs to be well understood by those who receive it before they can pass it on to their prospective pupils. To be able to rid yourselves of some of the tensions that encourage disease will be a good starter, so we hope we will have set the ball rolling in some small but effective way.

Personal Discovery Progress Chart

	SYMBOL OR ASSOCIATION	EXPLORATORY EXPERIENCE	COMMENT
GOD SYMBOL:			
ARCHETYPE:			
PERSONAL SYMBOL:			
POLARITY: Positive/Active/Yang: Negative/Passive/Yin:			
COSMIC ORIGIN:			
ELEMENT: (Air/Fire/Earth/Water)			
ANIMAL:			
FLOWER:			
TREE:			
COLOUR:			
NUMBER:			
STONE:			
METAL:			
MUSICAL NOTE:			

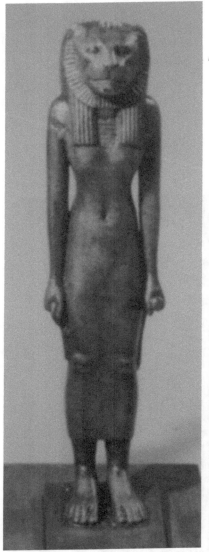

SEKHMET (Egyptian)

MIHOS: Lion God, son of Bastet (Egyptian)

WADJET (WADJED)
(Egyptian)

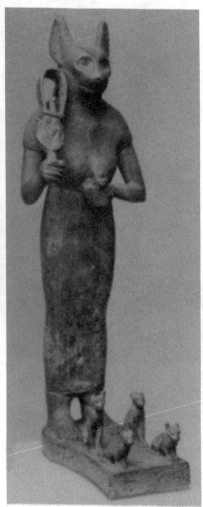

BASTET
(Egyptian)

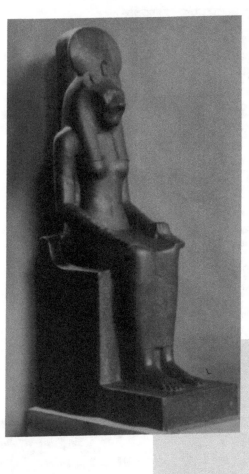

SEKHMET
(Egyptian)

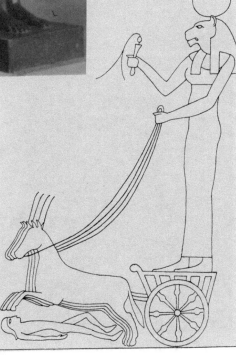

ASHTORETH
(Babylonian)

TEFNUT
(Egyptian)

THE LION GODS OF YESTERDAY AND TODAY

PART II

THE EVIDENCE

An analysis of historical, scientific and sociological factors
which tend to substantiate the Paschat teachings.

PART I

BEHAVIOUR

INNER AND OUTER TIME

Let us leave the Paschats and their communications at this point and, starting with the nature of Time, take a logical look at some of their claims in the light of existing knowledge from established scientific sources on the one hand, and speculative metaphysics on the other.

In his popular work, *A Dictionary of Symbols,* the Spanish psychologist C. E. Cirlot comments under the heading of 'Time': "Berthelot has noted that the time-pattern usually follows from the division of space, and this applies most particularly to the week. It was indeed the awareness of the seven Directions of Space (that is, two for each of the three dimensions plus the centre) that gave rise to the projection of the septenary order into time. Sunday – the Day of Rest – corresponds to the centre and, since all centres are linked with the 'Centre' or Divine Source, it is therefore sacred in character. The idea of rest is expressive of the notion of the immobility of the 'Centre', whereas the other six Directions are dynamic in character. At the same time, the 'Centre' of space and time also retains a spiritual significance. As Elkin has said, 'It must not be thought that the mythic era is now past: it is also the present and the future, as much as a state as a period.' Corresponding, in the strictest sense, to this zone within the circle, the 'Centre', is spacelessness and timelessness, or the non-formal, or, in short, the 'mystic nothingness' which, in oriental thought, is the hole in the Chinese disk of jade called Pi, representing heaven. As Eliade notes, *in illo tempore* everything was possible – species and forms were not fixed but 'fluid'. He goes on to point out that a return to this state implies the cessation of time. The idea that time – the week – derives from the spacepattern ought strictly to be discarded in favour of the notion that both time and space are the outcome of one and the same principle."

Time hypotheses have been incorporated into many past philosophies. The Gnostic ouroboros, or serpent devouring its own tail, for example, combines a paradigm of the time continuum with the composite symbology of all cyclic processes.

Metaphysically, time is postulated as being a positive force which is closely connected with the transmutation of energy into matter. Thought is also a creative energy which interacts with matter to produce form at the Inner Time level. Following the passage of time that brings death, that form is discarded and the thought, or intelligence that generates it, resumes an existence in Outer Time. In other words, it is no longer subject to the hours of the day, these being purely concerned with the 'frozen energy' state of Inner Time.

As somatic evolution slowly perfects, more 'ego-thought' energy is able to manifest through it until it is ready to accommodate a mutation. This may or may not be accompanied by physical phenomena, but it does generate a new mental ability to cope with concepts hitherto considered the region of superstitions, taboos, abstract thinking, etc. Eventually, the frequency of the controlling ego-thought energy becomes so intense that it can no longer accommodate the density of the molecular structure of that matter and so fails to effect a close atomic binding, by which time the planet in question would be nearing the end of its physical evolutionary cycle. But of course those essences or intelligences that have utilized its resources as evolutionary experiences do not cease to exist.

As energy slows down it coalesces into a more dense form. Becoming solid it thus occupies space, and in the act of occupying space it consumes the element of time, or rather uses the momentum of time to propel it forward in its evolutionary cycle. This very process is energy producing in itself.

Let us take the physical body, for example. It is born into the world of matter or solid objects, during which process it utilizes the facility of time. The friction of growth and physical move-ment against time causes a loosening of the molecular structure of that body, slowly effecting the process we call ageing. When the dominating intelligence withdraws, disintegration takes place and the molecules return to the sphere from which they were originally 'borrowed' – the four elements of Air, Fire, Earth and Water. This returning process can, of course, be hastened by cremation, and a cycle has been completed.

In other words, time gives definition and limitation to the material phases of overall experiences. The process of physical disintegration does not imply annihilation, all particles either being reabsorbed into other life forms, as with the poor soul who caught a cold courting in the old folksong "On Ilkley Moor Baht'At", or simply remaining as pure energy until such time as a newly acquired frequency is once again formulated. Inner Time can only exist where there is matter with which to make friction. In a state of pure thought all is timelessness. As I have learned from my later studies and communications there is, in reality, neither Inner nor Outer Time, only the ultimate state of timelessness. But one step at a time!

The cycles of Inner Time are by no means limited to this planet. Other celestial bodies also grow from youth to old age, disintegrate and change form when their molecular structure is altered through the influences brought to bear by the guiding intelligences responsible for their evolutionary cycles.

Space, like time, is allied to one level of experience only, i.e. the material or solid world. Space is really an illusion, although matter moves through it, or appears to do so as with the receding universe, while we also negotiate it in our everyday lives and advanced modes of travel. Once divorced from the context of matter, the mind may travel at the speed of thought to any cosmic frequency. A difficult concept for many people to grasp. In summary, time would appear to be a protective cocoon in which the chrysalis of the human soul can rest and develop.

I have included these few thoughts on the subject as I personally have found them helpful when assessing the Paschats' information.

The fact that the mind *does* function outside Inner Time has been evidenced on more than one occasion. Whether one cares to provide a logical scientific answer – and there is one as we shall see – or whether one still clings to the old ideas of clairvoyance, trickery, medieval nonsense or the like, is purely personal. In 1978 I was invited to take part in a BBC broadcast on Radio Four entitled *Arrows of Time*. There were several other contributors including my friend, Janet Augustin, psychologist and consultant astrologer;

Dr. J. M. Stewart of the Department of Applied Mathematics and Theoretical Physics, University of Cambridge; Dr. Peter Fenwick, consultant neurophysiologist; and Dr. Lyall Watson, biologist and writer. The BBC has kindly allowed me to reproduce some short excerpts from this broadcast and thanks are personally due to the interviewer, Leslie Smith, and to Dr. Watson for allowing me to use direct quotes.

As it was a long programme and absolutely packed with data relevant to this book, I had great difficulty in selecting passages of sufficient brevity to keep within the number of words allowed by Dr. Watson's agents, but I think I have managed to capture the essence of the message behind his contribution.

****

Edited extract from Broadcast on BBC Radio 4 recorded on Monday, 10th April 1978, and transmitted on Wednesday, 19th April 1978. I have chosen to lead into the broadcast at the point where Leslie Smith brings the conversation round to the realm of the metaphysical. The use of '...' indicates edited transcript.

[Author's Note: To keep my singing and writing work apart in those days, I used the pseudonym 'Athene Williams', in which name I was booked for all media work that was directly concerned with my psychic career. Later I shed that persona and reverted to the name I was given at birth – Murry Hope – a sort of return to roots, as it were.]

Leslie Smith: So called precognition, or premonitions, if indeed they do exist, are not necessarily an asset, at least as seen by Athene Williams who believes she's endowed with psychic gifts.

Athene Williams: I hope that scientists will solve this one for us in the future, but at present we don't appear to have conscious control over this faculty... What we really need is a set of coordinates with which one could tune into the appropriate point in the future. That would be fabulous... But we are still in the process of learning and I hope that perhaps science will be able to provide us with something like this in the future...

Smith: Do you think there would, in fact, be any value in being able to arrive at point so-and-so in the future?

Williams: I seriously wonder as to the wisdom of this.

Smith: Would you really want to do that?

Williams: To be truthful, no. I don't like doing it, I don't like seeing the future… I find it disconcerting and I think a lot of people could be mentally unbalanced by it.

Smith: Why is it that you don't like this particular capacity, which you believe you have, to look into the future?

Williams: Well, there is an old saying: "In the city of the blind the one-eyed man is king." As I see it, in the city of the blind the one-eyed man is *a heretic,* and heretics are never popular with the collective. Yes, I do find the faculty very uncomfortable to live with…

Smith: Athene Williams, who spoke a few minutes ago, got in touch with the producer and me to ask whether we had seen a television programme on the subject of time in which Lyall Watson was a participant. We hadn't seen it and were disappointed to have missed it. But later we discovered that the programme, in fact, hadn't been broadcast, and wasn't due to go out for several weeks. I wonder how Lyall Watson himself might interpret this.

Lyall Watson: We see time as a sequence – past, present, future – and in that order. But that isn't necessarily so: an event which takes place in space-time (let's not use the word 'time', but space-time). Let's view space-time as a pond. An event takes place: Kennedy is assassinated, let's say. This produces ripples, in this case quite large ripples in the space-time pond, because it affected a lot of people very directly. If one is approaching this event from the past, because memories of events in the past seem to be more common than they are of events in the future, we assume that it doesn't happen the other way. But I think one *can* remember the future. If one is in this space-time…

Smith: Remember the future?

Watson: Yes, if one is in this space-time pond approaching this event which is still to happen…

Smith: That's to say, your participation in the television programme, for example?

Watson: Yes. The ripples from that event are spreading out in all directions in the pond.

Smith: The event hadn't happened yet. Of course, we have seen it now and we enjoyed it, but at that stage the television programme had not happened. You hadn't met the other participants. It hadn't been transmitted.

Watson: Well, the evidence is that the ripples spread out in all directions in bigger and more noticeable ways into the future, but also back into the past. As you approach this space-time event – as you begin to enter the area of the ripples in the space-time pond – these are travelling at the speed of light, which is too fast for you to objectively appreciate, but something touches you, and you are aware of it. And as you reach the ripple the tendency, I think, is to sense it as a sort of touching – a fleeting experience – and because it isn't happening around you in real space-time, in your subjective terms, you think of it as a memory and file it away.

Smith: So, in other words, this is, simply put, a question of seeing into the future?

Watson: Yes, you can travel on along this axis into the event. You reach the event, it happens and you think, "Gosh, this is familiar, it's happened before." This is the déjà vu experience. "I think I've been here before." You *have* been there before! Now all that someone like Athene has to do in order to be psychic is to be able to bring that unconscious awareness of a future event into conscious awareness – to become conscious at the moment that the precursors of the event arrive. We all experience those precursors, but not all of us can bring them into consciousness…

Smith: … Why can't we all have this ability?

Watson: Well, why can't we all draw? Why can't we all play music?

Smith: Oh, you think it's an artistic thing, do you?

Watson: No, I think it's a personal thing. I think we're built in different ways. Some people are mathematicians and some are not. That's just how it is. You can learn mathematics and become reasonably good, but not everyone can be very good at everything. We have to choose.

Smith: So, according to your thinking, time is wrongly seen as something that is moving: it's a static band and we are the movers... Is that saying anything at all?

(At this point Dr. Watson introduced his hologram analogy which was longer than I am allowed to reproduce here verbatim. He described the unique three-dimensional nature of the hologram and commented how, if one were to smash a holographic plate into many pieces, each fragment, when subsequently illuminated, would contain the complete 3-D picture that was on the original whole plate.)

Watson: ... So every fraction of that plate is the whole. In biological terms, every cell in the body contains all the information necessary to make a new whole. In temporal terms, and we're talking about time now, every moment in time contains information inherent in all of time.

****

In discussing recent scientific discoveries concerning the nature of time at a later point in the programme, Dr. John Stewart was fully supportive regarding its relativity to given conditions. Further evidence had also come to light from experiments carried out in the Soviet Union which considered the question of time as having mass and, therefore, being a force or energy in its own right. All very reassuring for our present study.

Regarding my own rather strange precognitive experience of Dr. Watson's television programme some weeks prior to its transmission, perhaps this was just a foretaste of my future involvement in the subject. However, it didn't strike me as being much different from numerous other 'coincidences' attributed to countless clairvoyants I have encountered over the years, most of which have been greeted with the customary scepticism. But somehow the prevailing climate of opinion regarding unusual mental functions is mellowing, especially amongst the younger generation, many of whom no longer avoid subjects that in former years might have caused them to be labelled as cranks, and seriously hampered their progress in a scientific or medical career.

SIRIUS

And now for the question of the the Paschats being from Sirius. One can hear the cynics saying: "They've chosen a place far enough away for safety. Now if it had been Venus or Jupiter the data from satellite probes would have made nonsense of it all."

But in the light of our revelations, would they? Surely, if all time-zones exist simultaneously there could conceivably be – in terms of our past or future – planets that have been or might be suitable for habitation by oncoming evolutionary strains or 'impulses', as the Paschat calls them.

The star Sirius has obviously held considerable significance for mankind since the earliest recorded times. The ancient Egyptians featured Sirius in both their religion and calendar, the dog days being reckoned from its heliacal rising. They called it Sothis and linked it with their goddess Isis and the zodiacal sign of Virgo. The Egyptians, however, were not the only ancient race to accord special powers to this stellar beacon. Dogon records telling its story go back into antiquity and the Dog Star has enjoyed many names and titles throughout the magical and religious history of our planet.

Let us take a brief astronomical look at this luminary. Sirius is a blue-white star in the constellation of Canis Major, and being only eight and a half light years from the Earth it is one of our nearer neighbours. It is the brightest star in our night sky, unless we are to accept a more recent discovery in the Tarantula Nebula. For the time being, however, we will give our enigmatic stellar companion the benefit of the doubt.

Around the middle of the last century the astronomer Bessel studied Sirius over a period of time and noted a perturbation in its movement across the heavens indicative of the presence of another body close enough to effect a gravitational pull of some considerable force.

117

In other words, Sirius wobbled! Yet, due to its extreme brightness Bessel could find no trace of a mass large enough to affect a star of this size. Some years later a very small white dwarf star was found to be circling Sirius and its orbital period was calculated to be about fifty Earth years. This second star, lost in the glare of its companion, became known as Sirius 'B', sometimes called Digitaria, and it has since been photographed.

Astronomers recently have learned more about the nature of white dwarfs; stars that do not give out much light but exert an enormous gravitational pull because of their dense atomic structure. A white dwarf is a star that has used up its lighter hydrogen and helium atoms and has collapsed, which means that the remaining material has become so densely packed that the nature of its substance hardly equates at all to matter as we know it. When atoms are compressed to such an extent the resulting mass becomes extremely heavy. Robert K. G. Temple tells us that a cubic foot of the surface matter of Sirius 'B' would weigh 2,000 tons and a match box full of the star's core material would weigh approximately fifty tons.

Some astronomers believe they have detected a third star in the Sirius system. A man named Fox claimed to have seen it in 1920; and in 1926, 1928 and 1929 it was supposedly seen by Drs. van den Bos, Finsen, and others at the Union Observatory. Then suddenly this elusive star seemed to make itself invisible. More recently, Irving W. Lindenblad, of the U. S. Naval Observatory in Washington, D. C., probed the Sirius system but failed to detect a third star, although he gleaned much additional information about Sirius 'B' in the process.

In 1976, Temple brought out his controversial and thought provoking book, *The Sirius Mystery,* in which he postulated that beings from the Sirius system visited Earth many thousands of years ago and were partly (if not entirely) responsible for the leap from primitive life to the high standard of culture and civilization achieved by the early Egyptians between the years 4500-3400 BC.

These theories naturally caused a lot of reshuffling amongst the hierarchy of the scientific establishment. Some experts acknowledged Temple's scholarship and the evidence upon which he based his theories, while others who were formerly sympathetic to space visitor ideas leaped neatly to the other side in fear for their jobs or reputations. As ESP and the borderline sciences slowly become safe areas to investigate one wonders for how long these savants will indulge their game of intellectual musical chairs before it is finally considered respectable to look further afield than Genesis or Darwin for alternative explanations of human origins.

Temple based his hypothesis in part on knowledge of the Sirius system possessed by an African tribe called the Dogons, who live in Mali. These people, he believes, are the direct descendants of those pre-dynastic Egyptians who could have witnessed the arrival here on Earth of aliens from the Sirius system, their information dating back to those early days when their ancestors received it directly from their galactic visitors. In what other way, he questions, could they have gained knowledge of the existence of the invisible Digitaria or the other details they have possessed for centuries concerning this distant system?

The Dogon religion and accompanying rites are built around their concept of the Sirius system. They considered Digitaria to be far more important than its larger and brighter companion, even though it was not visible to them. They also had knowledge of the third luminary which the Dogons called the 'Star of Women' (which Temple has designated Sirius 'C'), as well as a small planet in the system. Their tradition also holds that from this solitary planet came a group of amphibians who founded their culture and gave them all this information. There is considerable confusion as to whether this third 'star' was a smaller sun or simply a large planet, since this ancient African tribe also made reference to the 'Shoemaker's Planet' and a 'Planet of Women'.

Sirius, the Dogons believe, was simply a companion to the essentially 'male' dwarf star, the orbit of which was depicted by them as being elliptical. The fact that they had no access to the theories of Kepler regarding ellipses struck Temple as significant. Furthermore, the Dogons reckoned the orbiting period of Sirius 'B' around Sirius 'A' to be fifty years, which has again been found to be accurate by modern scientific calculations. They were also well aware of the massive weight of Sirius 'B' long before astrophysicists had postulated the existence of collapsed or dwarf stars.

Of course, there is a great deal more to Temple's book. His research and presentation far remove it from the hysterical approach adopted by some writers in this field who do little to advance the cause of genuine extraterrestrial research. We can, however, conclude that there is a thread of evidence, tenuous though it be, for supposing that Sirius is in some way connected with the evolutionary pattern and development of our planet.

The ancient Egyptians worshipped numerous deities, many of which date back to pre-dynastic times, while others, notably the Isian five, appeared after Thoth (Tehuti) had won his famous game of draughts with the moon which secured the five intercalary days that accommodated their birth and changed the duration of the year from 360 to 365 days. According to tradition this original group consisted of Isis, Osiris, Horus, Nephthys and Set. [See *Practical Egyptian Magic* and *The Way of Cartouche.*]

Sirius 'A' has always been associated with the goddess Isis and some modern scholars have linked Sirius 'B' with her syzygy, Osiris, who was, according to legend, overthrown by his brother Set. Could the Isis/Osiris legend be describing a series of actual events that took place in the Sirius system prior to the collapse of the Osirian (Sirius 'B') star, and how does the third star feature in this saga?

Sirius 'C' is sometimes linked with Nephthys, the hidden one, or with her son Anubis. There is a theory popular in Europe that, when Set usurped the Osirian throne and banished Isis and her baby son Horus, the wilderness to which they were sent could refer to another planet of harsh environment: Earth, for instance, during an earlier era in its development.

It is my personal belief that the now-spent Sirius 'B' represents Osiris, and that his spirit or the intelligence that originally ruled this star has now ascended to a higher plane, as the myth tells us, or 'moved to a time-zone or dimension nearer to the Centre', as the Paschat would say.

Another interpretation is that the Isis/Osiris episode relates to a cosmological drama, with Isis (the Mother) representing the Earth, being miraculously impregnated by the dead Osiris (Sirius' seeding of this planet) and giving birth to Horus (Mankind) who is obliged to fight ill-health in youth (the learning of self-healing) before he is strong enough to overcome the evil of Set (misplaced energy) and establish his father's kingdom on Earth (the spiritual maturity of *Homo sapiens).*

The memory of these events was handed down as folklore from generation to generation in ancient Egypt and among the Dogon tribe, to name but two sources. It is well to remember that the Heliopolitan Recension, or earliest recorded part of the *Book of the Dead,* was copied by scribes around 3500 BC and was then so old as to be unreadable in parts.

Arcane tradition also subscribes to the idea of a race of devas or archangels, often referred to as 'the Gods', the 'Old Ones', 'the Great White Brotherhood', etc. who hailed from some distant star, and were responsible for the formation and seeding of our own solar system. Even the Hebraic-Christian writings which form such an important part of western culture contain references to 'sons of god' mating with the 'daughters of men' and the existence of 'giants', a term which could refer to either physical or mental stature. Different cultures assign them different names, but in truth it matters not: it is principles that are important.

To return to our Paschat: it is not inconceivable that a race of beings could have existed (or still exists) on one of the planets described by the Dogon, and that prior to or after the collapse of Sirius 'B' these people, having achieved a high standard of technical development, were able to set forth on an interstellar journey that brought them to Earth either by chance or design. Dogon tradition tells us that the beings who originally came from the region of Sirius 'B' were amphibians, after the fashion of the Sumerian Oannes. There could be two explanations here: that these visitors were clothed in some silvery material that might have appeared scaly or fish-like to primitives unused to the textiles of an advanced technology; or that they were the Crystal People described by the Paschats as being very light and crystalline in appearance, with long silvery hair and little physical difference between the males and females. This may also account for the 'Planet of Women' references.

Over the years I have encountered quite a few people who feel close links with Sirius and, from what I have been told, there is one memory thread that links them all: that of creatures nearer in appearance to the animal kingdoms than to *Homo sapiens,* but highly intelligent, understanding and compassionate. All those who claim Sirius affinities with whom I have ever spoken or corresponded are drawn to felines, as were also the ancient Egyptians. In fact, a love for and understanding of the whole animal kingdom would appear to be a prerequisite for Sirius roots.

Cats were sacred to Isis, and Herodotus tells us that the cat goddess Bast was actually the daughter of Isis and Osiris and twin sister of Horus. We are back again to Kaini's twin story! In fact, one authority whom I have read is of the opinion that there is more behind the constant references to the leonine nature of the family of Ra in the Egyptian *Book of the Dead* than might be imagined at first glance.

By now many of my readers will no doubt be wondering what a Paschat does actually look like. As my husband, my friends, and I are able to visualize their appearance, the ancient statues of Sekhmet in the British Museum would appear to be reasonably good replicas.

To the terrestrially orientated astronomer all this must doubtless sound like a prize dance to the tune of fantasy, in spite of history's tendency to support the fact that many of yesterday's fantasies have become today's realities. Of course there is no proof, just as the Dogon had no proof of the existence of Sirius 'B' until technical advances enabled scientists to confirm these age-old beliefs. While on the subject of astronomy, someone is bound to ask how the Crystal People's planet escaped when the Sirius 'B' sun collapsed, causing a massive release of cosmic energy, and how were these people able to protect themselves against the destructive forces of the dying star?

This is a question we did put to our friends who explained to us that the Crystal People were considerably more advanced scientifically than the Paschats in their understanding of the nature of pure energy in its many frequencies. They possessed the know-how both to deflect destructive nuclear modes and harness these forces for useful purposes. Apparently the Crystal People worked in frequencies of which we are totally unaware at present and they assure us that ultimately all energy can be tamed and controlled by mind power. Each level of potential reaching into subtle dimensions *ad infinitum* can be effectively controlled by or from a higher strata. In other words, once the technique has been mastered energies that are faster or finer can be used to manipulate those which by nature are heavier and coarser.

But back to the Dogons. Perhaps these and other early tribes who shared their beliefs were correct and a stray spaceship did drop in and provide that enigmatical missing link. I have even heard talk of a certain gene that the "daughters of men" inherited from the "sons of god" that has been passed down from antiquity, missing a few generations here and there but inevitably surfacing and endowing its carriers with unusual gifts and a deep inner knowledge of the cosmic oneness of all life. Foolish notions? Perhaps, but I seem to have heard some respected person telling us that "when the world adopts the fool's beliefs he is no longer the fool", and there are rather a lot of us about these days!

To this writer's knowledge, there is still no satisfactory scientific explanation for the sudden appearance of the intelligent Cro-Magnon culture in the Neanderthal backwaters some 35,000 years ago. Perhaps in some future papers our Paschat friends will throw some light on this enigma and also tell us more about their own solar system and its history.

LION CONSCIOUSNESS AND
THE LAW OF SYNCHRONICITY

While it has been scientifically established that minute particles can communicate with each other over vast areas of space, Rupert Sheldrake, Ph.D.Cambridge, former Frank Knox Fellow at Harvard University and research Fellow of the Royal Society, who specializes in biochemistry, cellular biology and philosophy, has recently observed that this phenomenon is by no means limited to the subatomic world. Random groupings of cells, he notes, appear to correspond between themselves for the purpose of organizing into distinct colonies for specific tasks. Nor are communications between fish, birds and animals subject to siderial or spacial limitations, many species being capable of effecting instantaneous telepathic contact over immense distances. To these phenomena Sheldrake has applied the term 'morphic resonance'.

Taking these facts into consideration, the possibility of mental telepathy between ourselves and intelligences in other parts of the universe does not seem so farfetched. Looking at it logically, morphic resonance should apply just as much to human beings as it does to the aforementioned substances and other living creatures. And if this is a constant principle, which scientific research would appear to indicate, who is to say which amongst us is or is not able to negotiate or employ it?

Many who are keenly interested in seeking beyond the exoteric, either scientifically or philosophically, have lost faith in the ability of ordinary people to come up with genuine answers. Centuries of bogus or untrustworthy religious leaders, philosophers, scientists and politicians have caused them to look elsewhere for the answer to life's enigmas. These are the folk who, when told about a new discovery or philosophy, will enquire, "But where did *you* get it from?" Should you tell them that it was your own invention or that it was given to you by Mr. X down the road, they may curtly enquire, "Who do you think you are?" or, "Why, he's nobody!" the implication being that someone from their own background or culture cannot possibly come up with the right answers. "A prophet is not without honour, save in his own country and his own home," says the Good Book! How very true! But hint at the work of some learned professor, or hidden source of knowledge such as a Tibetan temple, Indian guru, apostolic personage, or medium entranced by an Egyptian priest from 3000 B.C., and the tune changes.

On the other side of the fence, there are those who staunchly proclaim that anything purporting to come from sources occult, religious, metaphysical or extraterrestrial must automatically be the ramblings of a deranged mind, a money making ego trip, or the disguised voice of somebody who hasn't the courage to stand up and say what he or she really thinks. With all this to contend with, anyone trying to introduce new ideas under their own name would seem to be in for big trouble from all quarters. By the time society has informed them who they are and who they are not, they would need to be very brave and confident people to carry their own banners.

Taking into account that I recorded the earliest of these dialogues in 1980, and have been adding to them ever since during the last, few years, a whole flood of information has surfaced which reinforces my belief that Paschats are most certainly *not* fragmented aspects of my Higher Self, Lower Self, misplaced frustrated energies, or anything of the like. The first confirmation I received from an outside source was through a young lady who, while sitting with a psychic group in Liverpool, had been visited by a Paschat and given a similar tale. Since then further confirmatory stories have flooded to me.

In the writings of American authors Brad and Francie Steiger, whose books include *The Star People, The Seed, Revelation: The Divine Fire* and *Gods of Aquarius,* it is postulated that our planet was visited in eons past by space travellers who were responsible for the missing human evolutionary link. This information apparently struck strong chords with many people who had similar childhood experiences to my own. As a result of public reaction to his theories, Steiger instituted a questionnaire designed to collect data that might reveal some common connecting threads. The results of this survey revealed many similarities between people who felt they had connections with other worlds.

These consisted of, among other things, unusual blood types, an attraction to crystals, very low body temperatures, extreme susceptibility to cold, hypersensitivity to pain, an affinity to the star Sirius, a sympathy towards certain animals, and many more.

After considering the data that emerged from Steiger's survey, I am left with little doubt that I fit into his 'Star Seed' category and that my essence is not of the hominid impulse.

But apparently I am far from alone. In several of my books I have thrown out veiled hints regarding a connection between Earth and the Sirius system, without actually mentioning aliens of any kind or communications therewith. Yet I have received letters from many parts of the world from people claiming Sirius connections who have either experienced a strong lion consciousness and have close affinities with felines of all kind, or feel strangely drawn to crystals. Nor are my communicators maladjusted dropouts; they are found amongst the highly qualified, professional classes in equal numbers to young New Age claimants. In fact, many of them have never mentioned their feelings to anyone else, including their nearest and dearest.

The Paschat's information regarding the role to be played by Sirius in the future of this planet is re-echoed in the secret teachings of the Hopi Indians of North America, who refer to Sirius as the 'blue star Kachina'. A recent article in a popular British magazine mentions the Hopis' age-old belief that people from the Sirius system came to Earth some 250,000 years ago when they deposited time capsules some of which, they believe, will be triggered off during the period from 1986 onwards.

Relevant works by other authors have also come to my notice. *The Lion Path,* whose author is a distinguished doctor of physics and mathematics writing under the pseudonym of 'Musaious', and Karen Kuykendall's Cat Tarot cards, with their accompanying story of a strange, mystical, feline-dominated world, are but two examples.

Many other well known and established occultists and psychics are also starting to effect Paschat connections. A friend of mine visiting a large conference in California collected some of the speakers' literature which she thought might interest me. One particular logo, which consisted of a stylized feline head from which energy lines or rays of light streamed forth, caught my eye. I wrote to the lady in question, Mimi Donner-Levine, whose brochure informed me that she trained at Columbia University College of Pharmacy as a Bacteriologist and Medical Technologist. Among other things she had organized an independent group of psychologists, psychiatrists and social scientists to research mind/brain personality and ESP factors. She also practises astrology and has lectured and taught at the United Nations, Seton Hall, Rutgers and many leading universities and conferences worldwide.

I received a charming reply in which Ms. Donner-Levine explained that the feline logo was actually a white tiger with blue eyes that had appeared to her in meditation, and which had "the wisest eyes one could imagine." Its message to her was a profoundly spiritual one encouraging her, among other things, to rely more fully on her own wisdom potential and less on book knowledge. Ms. Donner-Levine tells me she has since researched the history and legends of the white tiger and has discovered some interesting facts relating to its esoteric symbolism. Here we have yet another manifestation of feline wisdom illuminating and overshadowing an obviously brilliant and enlightened lady.

Another recent book, *Incredible Cats, the Secret Powers of Your Pet,* by experimental psychologist David Greene, outlines some of the very amazing facts that have emerged from a psychological study of feline behavioural patterns. Cats, Dr. Greene tells us,
"use extra-sensory perception to predict danger to themselves, their companions and their owners;
"perform intellectually demanding tasks so difficult that many humans could not accomplish them;
"give early warning of natural disasters;
"cure apparently hopeless cases of mental and physical illness;
"save people from apparently inescapable injury or death;
"trace down their owners across thousands of miles;
"survive accidents that would spell certain death to almost any other creature;
"communicate eloquently, with other animals and humans, by means of a complex language of sounds, movements and odours."

Greene cites several near-miraculous incidences of healing received from felines and explains how the cat's ability to soothe and comfort sick minds and bodies is now being recognized in therapeutic centres in many parts of the world. He first observed the beneficial effect of cats while working with mentally sick and socially deprived youngsters, and his book is packed with scientific facts and clinical observations to support all that he has to say.

Joseph Wylder, another researcher into animal telepathy, states in his book *Psychic Pets* that the cat is the most psychic of all creatures and designed for total awareness.

If felines have this much to offer in their less dominant mode here on Earth, consider the potentialities of a highly evolved form of their species: the Paschats, for example.

At the conclusion of a seminar I was conducting recently in Yorkshire I was approached by a medium who works in close cooperation with a Dutch psychiatrist. While sitting with her group, she and another psychic present experienced a vision of a beautiful, ethereal-like lion (reminiscent of C. S. Lewis's 'Aslan', although neither party was familiar with the *Narnia Chronicles)*. The background of the vision was an arid desert across which the creature bounded gracefully. Grass, trees and a profusion of beautiful flowers sprang forth wherever its feet touched the ground and the accompanying message, which was registered quite clearly by several members of the group, was: "The Leonic Ones are coming, we bring joy and love and will be with you soon to help you."

There have been many incidents during and after Paschatinspired lectures I have given when established and reliable psychics present have noticed something 'different' about my contact. On one occasion I was approached by two very puzzled young women who hesitated to put their question to me. Finally curiosity overcame their embarrassment and one timidly enquired: "Tell us please, Miss Hope, why is it that while you were talking your face changed completely. We both saw it, didn't we?" The other lady nodded in agreement.

"That is quite normal when one is being overshadowed," I replied.

But her friend pursued the question. "Yes, we know that, we've seen it happen before. But why did your face look like a *lion's* and not a person's?"

I smiled and explained about the Paschats.

Two other ladies I have met recently confided in me that they had Paschat contacts, but until our paths crossed had found no-one else with whom they could share this information. Just two more of many similar incidents of Paschat awareness outside my own that I have encountered since my return to the public platform. The Paschats obviously have a profound knowledge of human psychology which is why they are able to effect morphic resonance with many people in the world today.

Following the publication of *The Way of Cartouche* in the United States letters have poured in thick and fast and several correspondents were quick to pick up my hints about Sirius. Although there is no mention in the book of Paschats or anything resembling them, I have received several letters from people who have a far memory of being something other than a hominid, but who have been too shy or embarrassed to tell this to anyone else. Among these were two people with distinct Paschat memories, and another who recalls "being a Plant Person on a planet in the Sirius System who could take up roots and move at will."

There has been no previous connection whatsoever between myself and these people who have contacted me, my Paschat writings being unpublished at the time. They have arrived at their own conclusions or drawn their memories from their own subconscious, or the collective unconscious of the Paschats/Crystal People.

It would appear that adults are not the only ones drawn to the concept of feline helpers from outer space. The American cartoon serial *Thundercats* (the existence of which I have only recently become acquainted with) also spells this theme, and it apparently enjoys great popularity among children on both sides of the Atlantic!

No, there are far too many Paschats about now for them to be purely figments of my own or anyone else's imagination. The lion theme is slowly merging into the collective unconscious of *Homo sapiens,* but then surely that is as it should be in accordance with the Law of Synchronicity, especially if we from this small blue planet are destined to have knowledge of and ultimately meet with the denizens of other time-zones.

All in the mind, is it? Well, perhaps we may take comfort from the words of Albert Einstein: "Imagination is greater than knowledge!"

DREAMS AND TIME SLIPS

Dreams would appear to be one of our primary connecting links between Inner and Outer Time, supplying a mountain of evidence to support the Paschat's time theories. While Jung's concept of a subconscious storehouse of information ripe for the picking could also apply, the time-zone idea holds good in many cases.

Mankind has benefited considerably from the visionary sleep of past dreamers: Frederich August von Kekule (18291896), Professor of Chemistry at Ghent, dreamed of atoms, snake-like in appearance, one of which seized its own tail suggesting to him the structure of the benzene ring that revolutionized organic chemistry; Elias Howe's dream of natives throwing spears, each of which had an eye-shaped hole at its tip, led him to place the eye of the needle at the point when creating the sewing machine; and Einstein's relativity concept came to him while he was dozing on a sick bed. Plots for stories by famous authors have also emerged from dream sequences; one could go on.

It is interesting to observe that in most of the cases, where dreams have influenced inventions or creativity, ideas are often conveyed symbolically, as though the subconscious mind has a language of its own. Jung observed this idiom to be universal, which led him to formulate his famous concept of archetypes. He wrote: "The sign is always less than the concept it represents while the symbol always stands for something more than its obvious and immediate meaning. Archaic remnants I call Archetypes or primordial images."[1] The secret of the success of dream interpretation, therefore, lies in understanding and translating those symbols. In the aforementioned cases, the people in question were able to relate their dream language to the projects on which they were working, or to the solutions they were seeking.

---

1   *Your Dreams and What They Mean,* Nerys Dee, p.61

Further evidence of varying time-zones can be gathered from experiences undergone during sleep state. I used to have an old alarm clock with the irritating habit of making a loud click about five seconds before it went off. I have often half consciously heard that click and thought to myself, "Oh, dear, time to get get up," but pulled the bedclothes over my head in the hope that it might not really be so. In those few seconds I have experienced dreams that would have taken several hours to re-enact in Inner Time before being rudely awakened by the alarm bell on the offending timepiece.

Sleep patterns are said to fall into two main categories. These have been given different labels by the various research establishments, but what we are basically dealing with is NREM (Non-Rapid Eye Movement) sleep and REM (Rapid Eye Movement) sleep. It is generally believed that we experience the deeper, more significant type of dream during the REM cycle, while NREMs tend to produce dream sequences of a more mundane nature. By the time this book reaches the public, however, new information on the subject will no doubt have come to light and we will be required to adjust our knowledge accordingly.

From a metaphysical standpoint dreams can be divided into those that are purely reflections of daily events or safety valves against life's frustrations and repressions on the one hand, and experiences that are in no way connected with our present day lives and circumstances on the other. The latter could well qualify under the heading of 'involuntary astral projection'. This is a subject in itself and I only want to touch on it inasmuch as it concerns time, for example those experiences undergone in REM sleep which obviously relate to other time-zones. These dreams may simply be permutations of Inner Time experiences, or they can throw up ideas and situations that bear no relationship to anything in the more familiar time circuits that form part of our ordinary, conscious everyday lives.

Sometimes when dozing, but not quite asleep, we may undergo the experience of walking towards a step or incline, missing our footing and falling, which sensation is usually accompanied by an involuntary jump known as a myoclonic jerk. Clinically this is caused by a sudden adjustment of the neuromechanisms in the brain, but the more metaphysically inclined amongst us might see it as the spirit returning to its body rather too rapidly.

A few years ago I was involved in a radio programme about dreams. Following the broadcast I was approached by an eminent professor of science and his wife who wished to speak to me privately. These were a devoted, well-integrated elderly couple whose grown up children and grandchildren were happy and successful. No anxieties or family disharmonies marred their advancing years and yet, in spite of all this, the lady told me that she constantly dreamed of another existence in which all was awry. In this worrisome dream life her much loved and devoted sons had turned on her and she had experienced disgrace, poverty, infidelity, and lack of love from family and friends. In reality none of these things had ever happened to her, nor were they ever likely to.

Her husband was greatly perplexed as he explained to me, "Mother and I are so close. Why should she dream such dreadful, unhappy things?"

"Did she find that the dreams influenced her daily life at all? Did they cause depressions, for example?" I enquired.

She told me they did not, nor did they ever cause her to doubt the love and integrity of those around her. But there were sometimes occasions when the border between the two worlds became slightly blurred so that she wasn't really sure whether she had, in fact, lost a certain item or needed to reply urgently to a distressing letter. One could only conclude that because her normal daily life was not affording her the experience of certain sufferings she was subconsciously creating these stress patterns, and experiencing sadness, horror, lovelessness and disgrace through her dreams. Just as the hungry, despised person often dreams in a compensatory manner or exalts some belief or ideal as an answer to suffering, so the over-compensated individual would appear to do the opposite and create tensive conditions in a timezone existing concurrently with his or her present one.

Sometime later I caught the tail end of another broadcast on the subject of dreams. The psychologist being interviewed, whose name I missed, was convinced that dreams come to us as warnings of impending events. The case was cited of a man who dreamed of the death of his much loved father, but the old gentleman was hale and hearty at the time and continued to be so for a while. But when the father did eventually die rather suddenly the dreamer found it far less traumatic, which he put down to having already undergone the emotional shock in dream state; an interesting observation in the light of our time studies. Do the experiences in one zone of time help us to cope with painful events in another?

A few years ago I found myself, like the professor's wife, experiencing a parallel existence in sleep state. Failures that had never occurred, sicknesses I have never had, decisions I had never faced; all came and went. I even dreamed of an attempted suicide that was prevented by someone's timely entrance. Sometime later I encountered a young woman I had known earlier in my life, whom I shall call Eileen, who told me a strange story.

A difficult emotional patch through which she had been passing had prompted her to try to take her own life. After downing a stiff drink to give her the necessary courage she had sat down on her bed and reached for the necessary implement, but a sort of drowsiness overcame her and she found her movements impaired. Suddenly, she said, the door burst open and I rushed in shouting: "Eileen, what do you think you're doing?"

She was so shocked that she dropped the razor, collapsed on the bed in tears and promptly fell asleep. When she awoke the next morning she felt, to quote her own words, "awfully foolish" and proceeded to pull herself together and get her life straightened out. I asked her to describe the room and circumstances. Her description was identical to the suicide episode in my own dream which had occurred around the same time.

Here we have an example of intertwining time-zones involving both the group consciousness and one psyche learning vicariously through the suffering of another. Perhaps ultimately we all experience with and for each other, knowing the other's pains, loves, trials, tribulations and jubilation, and that this participation eventually encompasses all life forms, both sentient and otherwise. Food for thought, indeed! Dreams, it would seem, may afford the evolving psyche the opportunity to investigate alternative experiences in parallel universes or other time-zones, thus alleviating the necessity to undergo too many variations in any one lifetime. While the body provides the Inner Time anchor the mind is free to roam in Outer Time to examine and. savour permutations of existence external to the immediate.

Time slips, however, are by no means limited to the REM mode. In fact, they can occur totally unexpectedly under very normal circumstances and when one is very much awake. When I originally read the Misses Moberley and Jourdain's well documented time slip story, *An Adventure,* I noted an interesting point amongst the impressions received by these two English ladies during their famous vision of 1789 events in the Trianon of the palace of Versailles. They described a feeling of overwhelming depression or heaviness which seemed to assail them. Miss Moberley commented: "Everything suddenly looked unnatural, therefore unpleasant; even the trees behind the building seemed to have become flat and lifeless, *like a wood worked on tapestry.* There were no effects of light and shade, no wind stirred in the trees. It was all intensely still."

There have been past instances in my own clairvoyance when I have tried to make my scenes come to life, but without success. There have been places, faces, objects, etc., but all were still and lifeless, like pictures in a book. But in spite of this these impressions have often proved to be quite accurate. One interesting observation, however: sequences of this kind always seem to relate to the planet upon which we now exist, its history or future, and never to time circuitry beyond the Earth.

But if, as we have been told, all time exists simultaneously there must be some preconditioning, either conscious or unconscious, that limits us to perceiving what was or will be. As our concepts of the universe are being slowly broadened by the horizons of science and transcendental awareness, so the mind becomes capable of encompassing even broader vistas. But the wisdom of remaining firmly anchored in the Now is emphasized by the fact that imagination can run riot in some people causing them to fragment to the extent that they are unable to cope with the present. A well-known American Presbyterian preacher once described this condition as "being so heavenly minded that one is no earthly good!" As I see it, these things are best tackled in very small doses, with plenty of earthing in between. Sometimes the trivia of day to day events can actually enhance our understanding of time, just as broad and exciting inter-time concepts can help us to cope more easily with the banality and boredom of repetitive living patterns.

The two time slip instances that I shall now relate involved neither clairvoyance nor ESP. The first of these concerned an elderly gentleman who lived in a small cottage on a large estate in Scotland which houses a very old and greatly historic castle.

Shortly after he moved into this cottage his eyesight started to fail and he found himself having to adjust his life to this slowly increasing disability. Being a country gentleman, he often took walks across the fields and on some days his eyesight was stronger than on others, depending upon the brightness of the light. One day he was feeling particularly fit so he decided to take a brisk walk across a part of the estate he did not normally visit. After covering several fields he came upon an old Scottish steading, complete with cottage, outbuildings, stream, and livestock.

"Strange," he thought, "I've never seen that farm before, how stupid of me!"

He noticed some figures inside the cottage and hailed them, but they appeared not to hear him; only the animals turned their heads and gazed curiously. He made his way back to the castle and called in, intent upon enquiring about his new discovery. There was no steading over there, he was told.

"But I saw it in great detail," he insisted. "In fact, I'll take you there and show you." So off they went.

But, of course, there was nothing – only open fields, undulating land and a running stream. Puzzled and somewhat mortified he returned home, but being a man of education and above average intelligence he declined to leave the matter there. In the ensuing days he made numerous enquiries and checked with former records in Edinburgh. Sure enough, there had been a steading on that spot in the eighteenth century, but it had been demolished some years later. The description, however, was exact.

Some months later a friend and I paid the old gentleman one of our regular visits. Without giving us any details he asked us to accompany him to the spot and say what impressions, if any, we received. Both my friend, who is also very psychic, and I independently described the same scene as he had witnessed. We were also able to add names that were later checked out and found to be correct. Our elderly friend had never previously displayed any psychic ability, being by profession a scientist and scholar, although it has been observed in other instances that an extra sense can be brought into play to compensate for impaired vision.

Time slips, therefore, can be effected by accident in some cases or by intent in others, but it is not necessary for one to be psychic.

My second story is a personal one in which the time slip occurred without prior hint or warning. One evening, as I sat before the fire, I turned on my radio to hear the weather forecast, but my clock was slightly fast so I caught the end of a programme that featured some ballet music by Tchaikowsky. Although at the time the subject of the ensuing experience was far removed from my thoughts, I was suddenly aware of being in a large theatre. The orchestra was tuning up for what I knew to be the performance of a ballet. The warmer air within the theatre contrasted sharply with the chill atmosphere outside and I could feel unwelcome draughts coming from behind me. I entered a theatre box accompanied by another man whom I addressed as 'Boris' and we were both attired in the dress uniform of a senior Russian regiment. A fair haired lady awaited us in the box, and her maid hovered just outside. The lady was peering across the auditorium through opera glasses as though eager to see who was present in the boxes on the other side.

The scene was so real I could actually smell a mixture of cigar smoke, unfamiliar food aromas, and heavy scents masking less desirable background odours. The whole experience lasted only a few seconds, but I was as much there as I was in the present. I was experiencing two time-zones simultaneously! Although I could see, hear, feel and smell the theatre and all that was happening therein, I was also fully aware of being in my flat, seated on the settee with my three cats, in the present and in full control; neither scene blocked out the other nor denied me access of movement and will.

In the light of the aforementioned, and many other instances which I have experienced myself or which have been cited to me over the years, the concept of all time existing in the Eternal Now becomes much easier to comprehend.

SYMBOLS: THE KEYS TO OUTER TIME

Taking a broad look at divination in its various forms, it would appear that over the centuries mankind has sought many keys to other time-zones, most of which have, as in the case of dreams, involved symbolic measures. Of course, people have been divining the future for centuries. The earliest races indulged in it and some former oracular utterances are well documented in classical history, notably the prophecies of the Pythoness at Delphi in ancient Greece. But it is in the area of interpretation that the problems arise.

It would appear that most of us have a subconscious monitoring system by which we reject as invalid any information that is likely to interfere with our karmic journey through the passage of time, or what we specifically feel we want to do at a given juncture. There are some people though who follow blindly whatever they are told and if it wasn't a seer they were consulting but a salesperson or a cleric, the response would be identical. In time travel, or any method employed for looking into the future, accurate descriptions of sensations or scenes are dependent upon the brain's ability to convert subconscious symbology into recognizable terms of reference.

So, if a psychic tells you that you are about to take a journey across the water in the company of a gentleman, pestering him or her with trivial questions about minute details is useless as these inter-time impresssions are often fleeting and cannot be sustained. One simply passes them on for what they are worth. Readings that deteriorate into cross-examinations or inquisitions only encourage the defensive accommodating embroidery that so frequently blurs or obscures the true issues. Hasten the day when people can time travel for themselves without the need for recourse to the time probes of others!

The effect of the passage of time on our lives, as described by Kaini, is very much in evidence from past observations. Here is an actual example of its effects on the life of one individual.

Back in the early nineteen sixties, when I was running a healing group in London, a lady came to us for help. She was about thirty-six years old, in a bad state of nerves and needing to unburden herself. Her story was not an unfamiliar one: a relationship with a married man. We all know the drill – he couldn't possibly leave his wife with the children at that delicately poised age between childhood and adulthood, but he would "get round to it eventually." Meanwhile, he enjoyed the fruits of both worlds. To add to her plight, this poor lady was living in very damp and unsatisfactory accommodation and was unable to find another rental she could afford. But her most pressing worry was that she would soon be too old to have the child she so longed for.

After counselling her for a few sessions, it so happened that I had to take off on a long tour with the major opera company with which I was then under contract, so I was obliged to leave her in the capable hands of the other members of the group. When I returned some months later she had gone on her way and I did not see her again until 1978 when our paths accidentally crossed. Although years had passed I still recognized her when she approached me and jovially I enquired how things were, fully expecting to hear that all her old problems were satisfactorily resolved. But no! She faced me sadly and answered, "Awful!"

Somewhat perplexed I asked, "Surely you're not still in that damp place, or did that horrid man let you down in the end?"

She gazed at me vacantly for a moment. "What damp place? What horrid man?" Then the light of recollection slowly dawned. "Oh, good gracious no, I finished with him years ago and married a very nice doctor. We have a lovely house in Surrey."

I was puzzled. "Then what *is* the problem?"

"It's my son," she complained, "he's in with bad company and I'm sure he's taking drugs."

"Your *son*? But the last time I saw you your big fear was that you'd never have any children."

"Oh, that's all past now, dear," she replied, dismissing my confusion with a wave of her hand. "My problems are quite different today – but just as worrying!"

In those earlier years I had spent much of our healing hour trying to explain to this lady that the difficulties she was experiencing at the time would all work out for her in the future. But she would have none of it. "How could they?" she protested.

I couldn't tell how; all I knew was that they would.

I think it was Bergson, in his book *Time and Free Will,* who wrote about the idea of the time curve that allows for precognition, but sometimes our view round the bend affords us such a fleeting glimpse that we are at a loss to colour it with the detail the enquirer would like. Perhaps it is better left unsaid, as the more orthodox thinkers amongst us advocate. Or should we strive for a deeper understanding of those conditions that would appear to govern our very lives? Curiosity is a driving force behind human existence. Acceptance may offer a closer and securer stronghold against life's seeming injustices, but there are other more truthful answers that seek out the cause rather than deal with the effects. Emerson's famous words about God offering to every man the choice between truth and repose – "take which you will, you may never have both" – may well be good advice!

Astrology is one study that reflects the inner nature of time with some practical degree of accuracy. Kaini, in one of his long private conversations with us, referred to birth charts as being like cosmic clocks that register at given times; striking, chiming, ringing, or slowing down as the mechanisms of our existence are triggered off by planetary movements. Their alarm bells ring when difficulties lie ahead, they chime for our happier moments or, like the single bell, toll at our parting. I have made a personal study of astrological transits in particular and find they never fail to set some lesson in motion, be it conscious or unconscious.

There would also appear to be connections between astrological charts, indicative of pockets of group consciousness time-travelling together much along the lines of Kaini's 'group entity' concept. Perhaps we commence our time travels in a kind of family formation, although the word 'family' could give the wrong impression if we think of it consanguinely. Regression also adds to this idea, as several researchers have found, and most of us would probably agree that as we proceed through life we do appear to recognize others of like mind or with whom we feel positive affinities. The opposite can also apply and, as the Chinese proverb so wisely tells us: "Destined enemies always meet in narrow passages.", Our errors are re-echoed across time until expiated by realization.

It may be observed that some skilled time-probers (clairvoyants, crystal gazers, scryers, rune readers, etc.) find it easier to work with one time-scanning system than another and it would be logical to ask why this should be if time has such universal implications. Perhaps an inter-time search might disclose that we learned the runes in old Scandinavia, the cards in a mediaeval gypsy encampment, or astrology from the Chaldeans. But even this might not be the whole truth, as we could well have brought our understanding over from some far-flung star and simply adopted those symbols relevant to the time-zone we first encountered on this planet Earth.

Many of the public at large are instinctively wary about such things as tarot cards or runes, feeling that there is something 'unholy' about them. No doubt the accumulated overlays that have manifested through systems of this sort must be felt to an extent by those who are very sensitive but wary, while the symbology has become encrusted with some rather questionable energies down the ages; enough, in fact, to obscure many of the original meanings and misguide the uninitiated.

This was of some concern to Kaiwi and Mikili, so when it was suggested to me that I invent a simple system that would serve both for divinatory purposes and subconscious contact, I reached back as far as possible in linear time to the earliest symbols used in ancient Egypt, as I felt these to be the nearest to the old Atlantean (and cosmic) originals. With help from the two Paschats I developed the Cartouche cards which have built-in spiritual and psychological safety valves, the idea being that anyone can use them without fear of attracting unspiritual energies. *The Way of Cartouche,* a hardback book which gives full explanations and instructions, and is accompanied by a set of cards, is now on sale in many parts of the world. The dedication in the front of this book reads:

"To my Leonine Teachers
for whom Time holds no frontiers,
with Love and Gratitude."

The Leonine teachers are, of course, my friends the Paschats, Kaini and Mikili.

Consideration should be given to the ethics of time-probing into the future, particularly where methods other than those employed in mundane divination are concerned. Hypnotherapy is a prime example. The lady hypnotherapist who helped me to remember – I shall call her Mrs. C. – once recounted to me an instance of progression during which the client (at her own request prior to the commencement of the session) was questioned regarding future events involving a certain locale. The answers given were far from satisfactory, however, and the conclusion later reached was that, when faced with a situation it did not wish to reveal in entirety, the subconscious mind becomes wily and uses numerous ploys that contrive not to give too much away. At which point these resistances are encountered and the ethical code involved requires further investigation.

The work of Dr. Edith Fiore, a Californian psychologist, who turned from specializing in general psychiatry to hypnotic regression, would appear to confirm many of Mrs. C.'s experiences. Clinical symptoms exhibited under regression involved significant changes in body chemistry, blood pressure etc., as would normally only result from moments of high stress, tension, terror or extreme suffering.

Some researchers are of the opinion that the hypnotic state functions best at a brain wave amplitude of five cycles per second. Dr. Helen Wambach, in particular, employed this measure in a biofeedback programme with one of her experimental groups. She noted that when answers to questions came rapidly the im pulses were from the right area of the brain. In instances where there was a time lag between questions and answers, the con scious ego had time to speculate and interfere on a rational basis, which involved the left hemisphere. So perhaps the blocking mechanisms encountered by Mrs. C. were not so much subjoin scious, as logical. More research in this area is necessary before any hard and fast rules can be applied either to the use of these obscure cerebral mechanisms or to the ethics involved therein. There are still conflicting schools of thought regarding the separate functions of right and left brain hemispheres, but these will no doubt be resolved satisfactorily by researchers in the not too distant future. Meanwhile, the general concensus of opinion is that Outer Time mechanisms in the human brain have connections with the right hemisphere, while rational thinking is a function of Inner Time as expressed through the left hemisphere. It would not, therefore, be illogical to postulate that our brains were specifically designed to accommodate a knowledge of other time-zones and a balance between the functions of both hemispheres, as with my own Russian bilocation experience, should be quite normal and not give rise to any traumas or psychological maladjustments. Only when this delicate balance is disturbed do we stray into the labyrinth of delusion and genuine intuition gives way to mental imbalance.

We walk the tightrope of reason across the abyss of ignorance in our never ending quest for knowledge and our pressing desire to penetrate even greater depths in the uncharted territories of human consciousness, so the Paschat is wise when he advocates plenty of practical grounding between mind expanding sessions.

TIME FOR THOUGHT

The Aquarian Age is spoken of as being the 'age of individuation', or a time in the history and evolution of our species when we learn to separate from the collective in a way which dispenses with the psychological need to adopt a militant approach against the established codes of those younger in spirit who still feel the necessity to shelter beneath its umbrella.

The process of maturation is ever a painful one, the normal growth pattern effecting the onset of puberty tending to produce rebellious and often anti-social behaviour. Later in life, when a more rational stance is adopted, the folly of these attitudes and their effect upon society usually becomes obvious. True spiritual individuation does not follow the pattern adopted by the physical world, but rather embodies a process of clear thinking, personal discipline, individual responsibility, planned acceptance of and cooperation with all other life forms with which we share this planet.

After studying Paschat philosophy and working with Kaini and Mikili since 1980 I have reached the conclusion that the message they are trying to convey is mainly concerned with forsaking the realms of spiritual adolescence and aiming for the kind of maturity that could prove to be the salvation of this planet.

The future of our civilization would certainly appear to be at stake. One does not need to be in telepathic communication with aliens to realize this; the evidence bombards us from all directions. Of course it would not be the first time in the history of Earth that an abrupt and tragic halt had been effected. Classical mythology supplies us with information about this fact if we care to look beyond the folk story mists that conveniently obscure their truths from less perceptive eyes.

The Paschats believe, as I do, that if order is to emerge from the chaos that faces us at present on this planet, we have to do some serious thinking and take remedial action before the other intelligences with whom we share this sphere take matters into their own hands.

What can we as individuals do to help the situation? If we strive towards personal individuation, will that immense struggle with the Self really be of any benefit to the world group as a whole? There is a flourishing market in self-enlightenment package deals: books, tapes and lectures purporting to teach us how to meditate, heal our own ills, forget our troubles and blossom into instant masterhood are well advertised. As someone who has been around in this scene for over thirty-five years, I find myself entertaining more than a hint of scepticism. While a New Age consciousness is obviously dawning and many people are striving for a kinder, more caring society, the casualty rate is frighteningly high, especially amongst the young. New freedoms that are not tempered by some kind of ethic, direction, or individual responsibility are causing a great deal of suffering, not only to those whose indulgences are the prime cause of their own condition, but also to the people around them who care, and to the flagging social systems that would appear to be fighting against immense odds to prop them up.

Surely what is needed is a programme of education that emphasizes both the personal vulnerabilities and responsibilities involved in self-discovery. One cannot fail to observe that many who seek to 'find themselves' end up discovering some less desirable aspect of their id, or lower nature, rather than their transpersonal or higher frequencies. This attitude is encouraged by certain sections of the psychiatric or counselling profession who laugh all the way to the bank while their unfortunate patients emit wild shrieks and animal noises in the cause of so-termed 'liberation'. Perhaps some do feel better afterwards, but then so does an angry petulant child who has just been allowed to smash a beautiful object in the guise of self-expression, which is another term for getting its own way.

In view of my comments it would be only natural to ask whether the Paschat exercises could not also be included in this category. I can only say from my own experience, as well as contacts and letters I have received from those who have already tried and tested them, that the disciplines outlined in this book present no danger whatsoever to the human psyche. In fact, they have an in-built psychological safety valve which restricts their effectiveness to the spiritual stage of development of the user. This means they cannot catapult the individual into realms that he or she is neither ready for nor able to cope with.

After working through the Paschat exercises myself I discovered many things of which I had been previously unaware, including a hitherto untried God Symbol and Personal Symbol. It took a lot of courage for me to break from the more orthodox occult tradition in which I had worked for so many years and put my faith in a new discipline, but I did it and can honestly say that the protection, help, care and love that I have experienced as a result has more than compensated for my earlier fears and insecurities. Paschat disciplines most certainly do work!

The main difference between the Paschat system and existing concepts of self-analysis would appear to lie in the dangers that are highlighted, the individual responsibility that is stressed, and the methods of externalization suggested to cope with and aid this achievement. A sort of inter-galactic thinking, if you like, that leaves limited Earth concepts of religion, metaphysics and humanism in the junior classroom and widens the general approach to far greater horizons than those conceived in past centuries of linear time on this planet.

This is not to say that all systems of belief were not correct in their time, but that we are now ready to think cosmically rather than parochially. Once free of the fetters of introversion we may find it easier to distinguish the wood from the trees and clear the cobwebs of superstition and prejudice that have blinded us for so long. The secret power of Paschat-inspired symbols would appear to lie in their detachment from existing Earth modes, which naturally frees them from the overlays of undesirable energies that have accumulated from the misdeeds and negative thought patterns of people over the centuries.

The new time consciousness demands a confrontation with the true Self and an encouragement to seek individuality as an important segment of the cosmic plan, while at the same time becoming aware of the connecting thread between that unique spark that constitutes the individual and the wholeness of the cosmic fire or godhead from which it originated. Thus individuating we may realize our natural potential for communicating with all forms of life and intelligence and our specific role in that timezone we call the future.

A knowledge and understanding of the true nature of timeenergy would answer many of life's enigmas. The concept of only one Earthly existence raises too many questions about unfairness, unequal distribution of resources, congenital illness, physical disabilities – one could go on – and does little to encourage peace of mind, understanding or brotherly love. As Kaini pointed out in the "Why Me?" chapter, there are answers if people could divorce their minds from the programming of past fears, dogmas and prejudices long enough to think clearly.

Many may still continue to complain about inequalities and why the people down the road live so well when they themselves are unsure as to where their next meal is coming from. But how many of us know the truths about the lives of those we envy? It would seem that there are problems at every stage and in every zone of time. A clearer understanding of the experiences time affords us as we pass through it could help to remove many of these resentments and jealousies. If we stop to think about it, much as we protest to the contrary, it becomes obvious that as soon as we have conquered one set of problems we promptly start searching for the next, and if there are none about we then create them.

We may move from our well established, comfortable and organized home into something more unusual, perhaps with a hole in the roof, bad plumbing, death watch beetle, and dry rot, but with 'such character and an absolutely marvellous view!' We then spend the next few years wrestling with our over-stretched finances and seemingly uncooperative workmen to get it all straight. Time passes and the dream house takes form, but by then petrol prices have soared so we cannot afford to run the car. And, being so much older, we can no longer walk the three miles to the nearest shops. 'Oh dear, we'll have to move back to town, such a lot of bother!' And so it goes. Time leads us by the hand from one set of experiences to another. Sometimes we lose our mental grip, but mostly we carry on until our bodies are worn out by their journey through time and space. Then by natural law we abandon them and move once more into temporary timelessness. But neither is that a state of permanency, so we keep on the move; sometimes backtracking or pausing here and there for a spiritual rest, but, as Kaini and his Teacher tell us, we eventually return to the Centre Point.

Perhaps someone more clever than I could produce a metaphysical paradigm illustrating time in all its complexities. Kaini has managed to convey the picture to me in a way that I can understand and I, in turn, have translated it as best I could. The ensuing years will, no doubt, fill in the missing pieces of the jigsaw as the light of science shows with increasing clarity that Time contains the key to many things, perhaps even the answer to the secrets of life itself.

The extent to which the Paschats have been able to express their knowledge through me has been governed by my somewhat philologically-limited memory data banks through which they have been obliged to search in order to effect the telepathic dialogues that have taken place. In many instances I have been unable to come up with the terms of reference appropriate to their message so it will fall to future generations to jettison many of the less suitable terms I have employed and adopt more applicable semantics.

Whether I am viewed as someone whose altered states of consciousness has led me to delve into the universal or collective unconscious, a psychic/sensitive who has been fortunate enough to make an interesting contact, or just plain deluded is up to the reader to decide. Let Thoth, Lord of Time, be the judge!

All I hope is that Kaini and his companions will continue to enlighten us, or endeavour to so do, for we sometimes feel like infants to whom some learned but kindly professor is trying to explain the mechanics of advanced nuclear physics in simple terms. But we do have sufficient faith in the human race (or some members of it, anyway) to believe that somewhere amongst the readers of this book there will be those who have the learning, natural intelligence, wisdom and intuition to develop this theme and take it much further, dare we hope, to the ultimate benefit of mankind and all other life forms within the universe, including Paschats.

BIBLIOGRAPHY

Arroyo, Stephen. *Astrology, Karma & Transformation.* C.R.C.S. Publications, Davis, California, U.S.A., 1978.

Bergson, H. L. *Time and Freewill.* Macmillan, London, England, 1911.

Dee, Nerys. *Your Dreams and What They Mean.* The Aquarian Press, Wellingborough, Northants., England, 1984.

Dunne, J. W. *An Experiment With Time.* Faber and Faber, London, England, 1943.

Green, David. *Incredible Cats.* Methuen Paperback, London, England, 1984.

Hope, Murry. *Practical Techniques of Psychic Self-Defence.* The Aquarian Press, Wellingborough, Northants., England, 1983.

Hope, Murry. *Practical Egyptian Magic.* The Aquarian Press, Wellingborough, Northants., England, 1984.

Hope, Murry. *The Way of Cartouche.* St. Martin's Press, New York City, New York, U.S.A., 1985.

Hope, Murry. *Practical Greek Magic.* The Aquarian Press, Wellingborough, Northants., England, 1985.

Hope, Murry. *The Book of Talimantras,* Thoth Publications, Loughborough, Leicestershire, 1987.

Hope, Murry. *Practical Celtic Magic.* The Aquarian Press, Wellingborough, Northants., England, 1987.

Hope, Murry. *The Pyschology of Ritual,* Element Books, Shaftesbury, Somerset, 1988.

Jung, C. G. *Memories, Dreams and Reflections.* Collins and Routledge & Kegan Paul, London, England, 1963.

Moberley and Jourdain. *An Adventure.* Faber & Faber, London, England, 1937.

Musaious. *The Lion Path.* Golden Sceptre Publishing, Berkeley, California, U.S.A., 1985.

Sheldrake, Rupert. A *New Science of Life.* Muller, Blond & White, London, England, 1981.

Sheldrake, Rupert. *The Presence of the Past.* Muller, Blond & White, London, England, 1986.

Steiger, Brad, *The Star People.* Berkley Publishing, New York City, New York, U.S.A., 1981.

Temple, Robert K. G. *The Sirius Mystery.* Sidgwick & Jackson, London, England, 1976.

Wallis-Budge, A. E. *The Book of the Dead, Vols. 1,* 2, & 3. Kegan Paul, London, England, 1901.

Wambach, Helen. *Life Before Life.* Bantam Books, New York City, New York, U.S.A., 1979.

Wylder, Joseph. *Psychic Pets.* J. M. Dent & Sons, Ltd., London, England, 1980.

Other titles from THOTH PUBLICATIONS

THE GALA DIALOGUES
Murry Hope

Have you ever held a conversation with the spirit of the planet upon which you live, heard her side of the story; her anger at the abuse of her body, and her feelings concerning that errant race we call humanity, large numbers of which she intends to jettison during the Pole Shift that will be precipitated by her approaching quantum leap? Hear it straight from Gaia herself as she tells all in a series of dialogues with fellow alien Murry Hope of *The Lion People* fame!

Read it if you dare – it shocks – it frightens – it defies all conventional esoteric, religious and scientific thinking!

ISBN 978 1 870450 18 8

COSMIC CONNECTIONS
Murry Hope

Following her series of dialogues with Gaia our own planetary logos, and inspired by the work of astro-physicist Dr.John Gribbin, Murry Hope has reached out even further into space and time and established a 'field to field' communication with the Controlling Intelligence behind our own Universe! Subjects covered by her information from this source to date include:
- There are an infinite number of universes, all functioning at different frequencies.
- All universes are conscious Beings fully aware of their cosmic functions.
- The role played by Tune in our own Universe's present expansion and eventual contraction.
- The fact that our Universe is actually a 'black hole' in the centre of an even larger universe
- The honing/refining role played by black holes
- The infinite process of birth, death, and rebirth via which the universe logoi themselves evolve through a process of continual change

And – wait for it – the guiding Intelligence behind our particular Universe is a 'she'

And there is a lot. lot more to come!

ISBN 978-1-870450-20-1

THE PASCHATS AND THE CRYSTAL PEOPLE
Murry Hope

Astounding revelations from another dimension of time and space, scientifically authenticated, covering: The impending Pole Shift; Cosmic genetic engineering?; The Quasi-crystal mystery; The cosmic virus that brought about the legendary 'Fall'; The role of animals on Earth; The role played by radioactivity in evolution; Science and the occult; and much, much more…

ISBN 978-1-870450-13-3

THE 9 LIVES OF TYO
Murry Hope

A story which can be enjoyed by both animal lovers and believers in extraterrestrials alike. Tyo is one of a very advanced race of felines, called Pashats, who come from a planet in another solar system. When allowed by his planetary neighbours, the Crystal People, to look in on Earth, Tyo is greatly distressed by what he sees and pleads with the Old Ones to allow him to travel to Earth to help humans and animals develop a better understanding of each other. The Old Ones grant his request and allow him nine lives on Earth as:

- a lioness in the Hall of Judgement in ancient Atlantis
- a Temple cat who is a favourite of Pharaoh Akhnaton
- a wild jaguar in the jungles of the Amazon River
- a little cat in Italy during the Black Death
- a pampered pet of Cardinal Richelieu
- a tomcat aboard a sailing ship in the eighteenth century
- a Bengal tiger during the period of the English Raj
- a self-sacrificing Russian Blue during the Soviet Revolution
- a much-loved Somali kitten in present-day Wales

During each life, Tyo meets many of the same animal and human friends albeit in different guises, for the relationship that binds them together transcends time. The atmosphere and historical events of each period, as seen through the eyes of Tyo are vividly described, while the feeling of his human and animal friends are also poignantly expressed. And therein lies the appeal of *The 9 Lives of Tyo* to people of all ages.

ISBN 978-1-870450-12-6